The Interrogation of
AMBROSE FOGARTY

The Interrogation of AMBROSE FOGARTY

a play in three acts

Martin Lynch

The
Blackstaff
Press

No resemblance to persons living or dead
is intended, either in the text or the
cover illustration.

British Library Cataloguing in Publication Data

Lynch, Martin
  The interrogation of Ambrose Fogarty.
  I. Title
  822'.914   PR6062.Y

  ISBN 0–85640–270–2

Published by The Blackstaff Press Limited
3 Galway Park, Dundonald, BT16 0AN
with the assistance of
the Arts Council of Northern Ireland

Printed in Northern Ireland
by Universities Press Limited

The Interrogation of Ambrose Fogarty was first performed at the Lyric Players Theatre, Belfast, on 27 January 1982. It was directed by Sam McCready and designed by Stuart Stanley. The cast was as follows:

Ambrose Fogarty	*John Keegan*
Willie Lagan	*Ian McElhinney*
Stanley	*Oliver Maguire*
Peter	*Derek Halligan*
Jackie	*George Shane*
Sergeant Knox	*Michael Gormley*
Constable Davy McFadden	*Brian Hogg*
W.P.C. Yvonne Lundy	*Susie Kelly*
Captain Levington	*Ben Benson*

Set in a police station in West Belfast, the play covers a three-day interrogation period.

Act One

The scene is a busy police station in West Belfast, Northern Ireland. At stage-right there is a cell and a door for another cell. The station reception area occupies stage-left, while an interview room dominates the centre of the stage.

At the reception area desk **Sergeant Knox** *is typing out a report. Behind him, Woman Police Constable* **Yvonne Lundy** *and a plain-clothes policeman,* **Jackie,** *are standing in a doorway, apparently watching television.*

The crackling of the station communications radio at the back wall dominates occasionally.

Radio   Echo Tango Eight One. Echo Tango Eight One to Bravo Hotel, over. Echo Tango Eight One. Echo Tango Eight One to Bravo Hotel, over.

Yvonne   Echo Tango Eight One, send, over.

Jackie   I hate that pansy bastard Russell Harty!

Radio   Registration number, Juliet, Oscar, India – five, nine, zero, seven. It would seem that there are three occupants, over.

Yvonne   Roger. Keep in touch with the DSO.

Radio   Roger, out.

(A plain-clothes policeman, **Peter,** *enters.)*

Peter   There's that report, Sergeant Knox. Have it checked out.

Knox   Will do, Peter.

Peter   Oh, by the way, what's the latest on the situation outside?

Knox   It would appear the main riot's over. We're down to about the last two dozen die-hards.

Peter   Any arrests?

Knox   None so far.

Peter   The Major seems to have handled things well.

Knox   Well, he's near the end of his tour, so he's seen it all before.

Peter   Almost a veteran, eh?

(Exits.)

Knox Yvonne!
 (**Yvonne** *presents herself.*)
 Put a call out to the vehicle nearest that location and have it checked out.
Yvonne Right.
Jackie Yvonne, come on and see the antics of this. He can't get the envelope opened!
Yvonne Sorry, Jackie, I'm busy. (*Speaks into radio*) Bravo Hotel, Bravo Hotel to Bravo Hotel One One, over.
Radio Bravo Hotel to One One, send, over.
Yvonne Would you check out a report of a single shot heard in the Cavendish-Oakman Street area, over.
Radio Will do. Do we know if there are any Army patrols in that location? Over.
Yvonne No Army patrols. Roger, out.
 (*Returns to the doorway.*)
Jackie That man is one silly nincompoop!
 (*The phone rings.* **Knox** *answers.*)
Knox Hello. . . Yes. . . If you call at 3 p.m. tomorrow, Mr Donnelly, someone will attend you. . . Right. . . Cheerio.
 (*He puts the phone down. Presently some shouting is heard from off-stage at the main entrance to the reception area. A head appears at the entrance, on the floor. The face is grinning broadly. As we see just a little bit more of the head and shoulders, an Army* **Captain** *swings into view with the legs of the body, and proceeds to trail it across the floor, kicking at it as he does so. The body is* **Willie Lagan**. *He is holding on to a brown paper parcel which is under one arm while he waves with the other. Unbelievably, he is still grinning. He shouts and whistles.* **Willie**'*s whistle is more a kind of tuneless hissing noise than a real whistle.*)
Captain Shut up! Shut up, mate!
Willie No problem, no problem. (*Whistles.*)
Captain I said, shut your beak!
Willie Get 'em up, move 'em out!
 (*Whistles again, then roars with laughter. The* **Captain** *drops* **Willie**'*s legs.*)
Captain Now get up, you lunatic.
 (**Willie** *turns over to a sitting-up position.*)
Willie Lunatic, lunatic – ahhh! I like it, I like it. (*Grabs the* **Captain**'*s baton*) Here, shake hands.
Captain I'll make you stand up.
 (*He proceeds to draw a baton and beat* **Willie** *once or twice before*

2

Knox *rushes out from behind the desk.)*

Knox   Just a minute, just a minute, Captain, that's quite enough.

Captain   He won't get up!

Knox   He'll not be able to get up if you keep that up.
(physically steps in between the Captain and Willie.)
Let's have you on your feet, Sir.
(Helps Willie up by the arm) That's better. Now what's all the trouble about?

Willie   He hit me a dig, a dig.

Captain   I'm placing this man under arrest for taking part in a riot.

Knox   Well, if you don't mind me saying so, Captain, he doesn't exactly look like the normal teenage rioter.

Captain   Well, he fucking well is. I want him charged.

Knox   What were the circumstances?

Captain   He was observed throwing bottles of beer, and when we charged forward we placed him under arrest.

Willie   That's lies, all lies.

Captain   I saw you with my own eyes!

Willie   I'm not talking to you, talkin' to this man, okay shut up.

Knox   All right, all right!
(A call comes through on the radio.)

Yvonne   Sergeant Knox! Constable McFadden requires assistance at the door to bring in a prisoner.

Knox   Right. Would you do that, Captain?
(The Captain moves to leave. Willie laughs.)

Willie   *(whistling)* Hold on, hold on! Where's my. . . *(whistles and mimics guitar-playing)* guitar, guitar?

Knox   Do you have some property belonging to this man?

Captain   Yeah, it's outside.
(Steps off and returns with a guitar.)

Knox   I'll take it.
(Knox takes the guitar and sets it down beside him. Exit Captain.)

Willie   Magic, magic. That's mine, that's mine. Try and guess who give me that. Don't know, don't know? Cash, Cash, Johnny Cash, big star, good singer, good singer.
(Sings)
'I hear that whistle blowin',
It's comin' down the line
I ain't seen the sunshine
Since I don't know when
'Cause I'm stuck in Folsom Prison
And time keeps draggin' on. . .'

Knox All right, that's enough, I believe you, Johnny Cash gave you it, all right.

(**Willie** *holds the guitar up and kisses it.*)

Willie I love it, I love it. That's my wife, my wife.

Knox Right, now. I want some details from you. What's your name?

Willie My name? Willie Lagan, Country-and-Western singer, that's me.

Knox *(writing down the details)* Lagan. Where do you live, Willie?

Willie With my mother. *(Laughs.)*

Knox I didn't ask you who you lived with, I asked you where you lived.

Willie The Lower Whack, Lower Whack.

Knox The what?

Willie Lower Whack, the Lower Falls, know. . . *(whistles)* am. . . a. . . Grosvenor Place.

Knox What number in Grosvenor Place?

Willie Ninety-five.

Knox Ninety-five, Grosvenor Place. Now, what's all this about you being involved in the rioting?

Willie I don't know, no idea, not me.

Knox Where exactly were you arrested?

Willie Exactly?

Knox Exactly.

Willie *(whistles as he points downwards, then swoops his hand down and grabs his own private parts)* Right there! Right there! Your man, General Montgomery, him, him. He grabbed me by the swingers. Sore, fuckin' sore.

Knox No, no, hold on. Where were you standing when you were arrested?

Willie Springfield Road corner, know just outside Beacon's Bar, right there. I never done nothing!

Knox Outside Beacon's Bar at the junction of the Falls and Springfield roads?

Willie Magic, that's it, that's it.

Knox What were you doing there in the middle of a riot?

Willie Just going home, on my way home. I was just walking. . . *(whistles)* down the Falls Road and *(whistles, hand down at his privates again)* arrested! I wasn't even. . .

Knox No, now hold on a second. Start from the start. What were you doing in that area in the first place?

Willie Right, okay. From the start, the beginning, Adam and Eve, okay. I was. . . *(whistles and imitates the actions of playing the guitar)* playing in the wee Dwyer's Club.

4

Knox That's the Dwyer's Club in Leeson Street?

Willie That's right, that's right, me, me. Every Sunday afternoon. Me, Willie Lagan, Country-and-Western singer. Live on stage, live, live! *(Sings)* 'I'm tired of crying, and all your lying. . .' Finished. . . *(whistles)* got x-rayed, know, money, and fucked off. . . *(whistles)* nipped. Up to the sister's, called up.

Knox Where's your sister's?

Willie Cavendish Street. . . *(whistles)* round the back. Sister gave me some soda farls, soda farls for my mother. I was walking home and. . . *(Whistles.)*

Knox Yes, but did you throw any bottles of beer at the soldiers?

Willie *(laughs)* Good joke, good joke. Is there no bar in here, no bar? *(Laughs.)*

Knox Somehow or other I don't think you're the sort that would throw away a bottle of beer for any reason. Right. I'm afraid I'll have to lock you up until we get to the bottom of this. If that soldier insists on pressing charges you could be in trouble. Let's go.

Willie Guitar, guitar, that's mine.

Knox Right. You can take that with you but not a sound, hear!

Willie Okay, okay.

> *(Lifts his guitar. He is led to a cell and locked up by* **Knox***. In the meantime,* **Constable Davy McFadden** *arrives with* **Ambrose Fogarty** *by the arm, escorted by the* **Captain***.)*

Davy Where's Sergeant Knox?

Yvonne He's just gone to the cells with a prisoner.

Davy *(to* **Ambrose***)* Right. Sit down there, would you please.

> *(***Ambrose** *sits down. The* **Captain** *stands beside him.)*

Give a buzz upstairs and tell the quare fellas the prisoner's here.

Yvonne *(buzzes)* Ah, Detective Scally, the prisoner's here. . . Right. *(To* **Davy***)* Put him in an interview room, there'll be somebody down right away.

Davy Okay. C'mon

> *(***Ambrose** *stands up.)*

Thanks Captain, I'll take him on in.

> *(***Davy** *escorts* **Ambrose** *to the interview room.)*

Captain Hey, Yvonne, tell us what colour your knickers are.

Yvonne I've none on.

Captain Way-hey! That's what I like to hear. A girl that's ready for action.

Yvonne You don't know what action is, Captain.

Captain Why don't you show me the ropes?

Yvonne   I'm not in the habit of wasting my time.

Captain   Na, you're more hung up on that fat bastard of a police constable that just walked out there.

Yvonne   I beg your pardon.

Captain   *(mimicking her voice)* I beg your pardon. *(Laughs.)*

Yvonne   If you can't hold a conversation without making fun of people, then you'd better not try in the first place.

Captain   I'm sorry, it wasn't me and I'll never do it again.
(Then moves closer and leans on the desk right beside **Yvonne**.*)*
Listen, Yvonne, darling, how would you like an offer you couldn't refuse?

Yvonne   Like what?

Captain   Like you and me going out one of these nights, eh?
(She moves away to the radio as a message comes through.)

Yvonne   I can't. I work. Golf Charlie Eight One, to Bravo Hotel, send, over.

Captain   What do you think I'm doing over here? Pheasant shooting?
(As the **Captain** *exits,* **Jackie** *enters the interview room, camera in hand.)*

Jackie   Right, who have we here?

Davy   Prisoner Fogarty.

Jackie   Ah, Ambrose Fogarty. I've waited a long time to meet you.
(Nods to **Davy**, *who leaves.* **Ambrose** *is silent.)*

Jackie   What's wrong, Ambrose? Not in the mood for talking? I see. Well, we'll leave all that till later. In the meantime, some formalities.
(Harshly) Stand up!
*(***Ambrose** *stands up.* **Jackie** *lifts a small blackboard.)*
Full name, Ambrose?

Ambrose   Ambrose Fogarty.
*(***Jackie** *chalks this on blackboard.)*

Jackie   Date of birth?

Ambrose   4th of the 11th, '53.

Jackie   Religion?

Ambrose   None.

Jackie   None at all?
*(***Ambrose** *shakes his head.)*
Well, for these purposes I'll just put down RC. Okay? Now just hold that like a good man and we'll get some nice wee pics of you.
(Places the board in **Ambrose**'s *hands up against his chest.)*
That's it, up a little, fine.

6

(As he moves back to take the photograph, **Ambrose** *lowers the board down by his side.)*
Hold it up to your chest.

Ambrose   No.

Jackie   What do you mean, 'No'? Hold it up!

Ambrose   I'm not doing it.
*(***Jackie*** *walks over to* **Ambrose***.)*

Jackie   Listen, Bonzo. You're not in a position to say what you're doing and what you're not doing. Now just hold that board up to your chest *(physically positions* **Ambrose***'s hands on the board)*, and no oul' nonsense out of you.
*(***Ambrose*** *drops the board on the floor.* **Jackie** *glares at him.)*
All right, we'll do it without the board.
(Moves back in position.)
Look into the camera, Ambrose.
*(***Ambrose*** *turns his head to the side and scratches the side of his head with the opposite hand.)*
What are you playing at?

Ambrose   I'm not having my photograph taken. Under the terms of the Emergency Provisions Act 1973, you need a certificate signed by a police officer no lower in rank than a Chief Inspector, before you can take a prisoner's photograph.

Jackie   Is that right? Well, let me tell you something, mate. You're not sitting at no Civil Rights meeting now. Nor standing at a street corner. You're in a police station, arrested as a suspect terrorist, and as such you have no rights. Now keep your hands down by your side and look into this camera.

Ambrose   I'm not doing it.
(As **Jackie** *positions the camera,* **Ambrose** *covers his face with his hand.)*

Jackie   Right!
(Puts the camera down.)
We'll see about that later on. Stand over by that desk.
*(***Ambrose*** *obeys.)*
I'm going to take your fingerprints.
(Organises some items on the table.)
Give me your right hand.
*(***Ambrose*** *remains silent and motionless.)*
I said, give me your right hand.
*(***Ambrose*** *shakes his head determinedly.* **Jackie** *grabs his arm.* **Ambrose** *pulls it back.)*

Look, don't make this difficult for yourself. You can co-operate with me now, or I can call in half-a-dozen soldiers to physically take your prints. Which way do you want it done?

Ambrose   I don't want to have my fingerprints taken. It's against the law.

Jackie   You know quite a lot about the law.

Ambrose   Enough to know that to have my photograph or fingerprints taken you need a Chief Inspector's certificate.

Jackie   Is that so? Right. If that's the way you want to play it, fair enough. If you're going to act the smart Alec, just remember you have three long days and nights ahead of you. If you want to mess us about, just think what we can do to you over three days.

(**Ambrose** *remains silent.*)

But then you seem to be a cocky character. Reckon you'll daddle through this, eh? Do you, Ambrose?

(**Ambrose** *shrugs his shoulders.*)

Well, let me let you into a wee secret. We allowed you to run about too long. Now, we have you by the goolies. All our evidence collected. Signed, sealed and delivered. You'll not walk out of here this time. Now c'mon till I bring you to your cell. You'll have to get used to life in an eight-by-four box. We'll get your photo and prints later on. No hurry. In fact, Fogarty, there's no need to hurry anything anymore, where you're concerned. Let's go.

(**Jackie** *and* **Ambrose** *go out into the main reception area.*
Knox, *by the radio, is discussing a point with* **Davy.**)

Sergeant, put this man in a cell, please.

Knox   *(to* **Davy***)* Put him in Cell Two.

Davy   Right.

(*Takes* **Ambrose** *by the arm.*)

Jackie   Oh, ah, Fogarty. Remember what I said. There's no hurry. No hurry at all. *(Exits.)*

Knox   *(into radio)* Bravo Hotel to Bravo Hotel Eight One, over. Bravo Hotel to Bravo Hotel Eight One, over.

Radio   Bravo Hotel, send.

Knox   Would you go to the assistance of an officer outside the BBC in Ormeau Avenue. Apparently there's a drunk man there who's knocked over two bollards of flowers and he's now kicking at the door of the BBC. You won't believe this, but he says he wants to make an appeal over the air to his wife, who left him last night.

Radio   It takes all sorts. Roger, out.

Knox   Roger on that.

(*While* **Knox** *has been using the radio,* **Davy** *has taken* **Ambrose** *to*

the cells, **Davy** *jangling a bunch of keys. He directs* **Ambrose** *to a cell.*
Ambrose *enters and turns.)*

Ambrose   You wouldn't have a paper on you, mate?

Davy   Sorry, I don't.

Ambrose   Could you get me one?

Davy   We're not allowed.

Ambrose   Right, thanks.

(With a loud slam, **Davy** *locks the cell door and takes up a position at the end of the cell block. He sits on a chair beside a table and begins to write on a clipboard.*

Ambrose *stands in the middle of his cell. He looks around. The walls are white, bare, except for one small ventilator up near the ceiling. A light bulb in a round glass casing glares down from high up on a wall. A few grey, army-type blankets lie crumpled on top of a single bed. A solitary chair rests in a corner.*

He makes a quick check of the cell door, then sits on the chair. He runs one hand through his hair and heaves a disgusted sigh.

Presently he jumps up angrily and paces the floor.)

Ambrose   Fuck this! Three frigging days in this kip, Jesus Christ! How am I gonna stick this? Fuck it, fuck it, fuck it. Tons to look at on the walls.

(He runs his hand along the wall, then checks under the mattress.)

Three days! Seventy-two hours! What to hell's it all about? Nobody has said a dickie-bird up to now, except, 'All our evidence collected'. What are they on about, what evidence?

(Pause)

What about Gerry? I wonder do they know anything about Gerry?

(Pause)

I wonder will I get my bollocks knocked in. They don't bring you in here for nothing.

(Stops suddenly.)

That was wild in the house this morning. Christine. Her eyes. You could actually see the terror in her eyes. Thank Christ the kids didn't waken. That soldier was one ignorant bastard. I hope she's got over it.

Scrub that. I have to stop thinking about her. Or the children, while I'm in here. From here on in I'm on my own. No distractions. Nobody to worry about, only me.

(He spots the ventilator up on the wall, jumps up on the bed and feels round it. He stops. A crafty grin spreads over his face.)

I wonder will I get away with the fingerprints and photographs thing.

(He jumps down from the bed and bursts loudly into song.)

9

'Heaven knows, it's not the way it should be.
Heaven knows, it's not the way it should be.'
(**Peter** *and* **Jackie**, *talking, enter the interview room.*)

Jackie   I felt like hitting him a dig in the jaw.

Peter   Not to worry. He knows as well as we do that his prints and pics will be taken. He's putting on a show of confidence.

Jackie   A show?

Peter   Don't kid yourself. Anybody who finds themselves arrested and thrown in a cell is worried. Worried sick, in fact. Some are just better than others at concealing it.

Jackie   So you're gonna start this psychological thing, eh?

Peter   That's what it's all about, Jackie. A battle of wits.

Jackie   I don't wear that crap. A good going-over is more than enough for most of them.

Peter   Yes, Jackie, but the *fear* of a good going-over is even worse. It's harder to penetrate a person's mind than their body, but once you do get in, they're yours for the taking.

Jackie   I'm not so sure about that.

Peter   The essence of interrogation is psychology. Look. When you hear somebody kicking up in the papers about Castlereagh and interrogation methods, what is it you hear? 'Brutality, punched, kicked, beat-up', etcetera. You never hear a word about the real interrogation. I've seen guys walk out of here, wrecked, who never had a finger laid on them. You can be sure Fogarty's walking about that cell with his mind on the boil. Like a bubbling volcano. It's our job to make it erupt.

Jackie   Have you came across Fogarty before, Peter?

Peter   Not face to face. But I remember during the UWC Strike in 1974, I watched him in Leeson Street for over an hour, out the back window of a Ford Transit van.

Jackie   What was he doing?

Peter   Remember there was a food shortage? Well, he and his mates had got hold of a load of bread and he was distributing it to the people. That's the sort of thing he would be seen doing publicly. Helping the cause by helping the working-class and all that stuff.

Jackie   Do you think he has any idea why he's in here?

(**Ambrose**, *in his cell, is lying on the bed. He sits up sharply.*)

Ambrose   I wonder is it anything to do with the Newry thing? Maxie? That was two years ago.

(*Grins.*)

Huh. That stew was woeful. No, it wouldn't be that.

What? What is it? If I knew I could attempt to prepare myself, but I don't frigging know!

Oh Christ, watch it, watch it, watch it. Take it easy, take it easy. Don't run away with yourself. Hold it, hold it. I have to hold my nerve. I've three days of this to go through. If I'm losing my nerve now, without a finger being laid on me, what am I going to be like if they start punching me? I wonder how I would react to a dig in the jaw.

(He prods his jaw with his fist.)

Strange. I've never been struck in anger by anyone in my whole adult life. Maybe I'll take it all right. You never know.

(He jumps up and paces the floor.)

On the other hand, I might end up throwing myself out of an upstairs window like your man from Ballymurphy. Or the fella who they *said* hanged himself in his cell at Castlereagh. Jesus Christ! What would have to be going on to allow that to happen? Reminds me of Chile. Santiago Stadium.

But then again, I might just walk out in three days' time as clean as a whistle. British justice and all that crap. It's the in-between that counts.

(He sits down on the bed.)

The not knowing. The uncertainty. The fear. The breaking-point.

(In the interview room, **Jackie** *and* **Peter** *continue their conversation.)*

Jackie   Of course he has a breaking-point. The back of his neck!

Peter   You're hell for this physical thing. I really don't think it'll have all that of an effect on this fella.

Jackie   You let me take him in hand and I'll show him. A good boot in the balls'll bring an elephant down.

Peter   It won't necessarily get him to sign a confession. No, Jackie. Better to let this man spend a lot of time in his cell worrying. The oul' volcano'll be bubbling away. And after each interview the lava'll get hotter and the bubbles higher.

*(***Ambrose*** is lying on the bed, trying to balance the heel of one shoe on the toe of the other.)*

Ambrose   Anyway, I'm here for a while, so I might as well make the best of it. A newspaper would come in handy. Big Geek said he was allowed newspapers. *(Smiles)* Bastard musta been giving information to them.

I wonder should I try and get some sleep? No. They're liable to be watching me. They'd probably wait until I'm in a deep sleep then

come and trail me out for an interview while I'm all groggy.
(He stands up and takes his coat off.)
Smicker says it happened to him. But you never know when
Smicker's telling the truth and when he's imagining things.
I don't care. They're not gonna break me. No talking. No signing
statements. No nothing.
*(He gets down on the floor and starts doing press-ups, then stops
abruptly.)*
I wonder do they feed you in here?
*(Yvonne enters the cells area pushing a catering trolley. She stops
beside Davy.)*

Yvonne Are you just going to sit there or do I have to squeeze sausages
and beans under the cell doors?
(Davy stands up sharply.)

Davy Ready whenever you are.

Yvonne Sorry for waking you out of your sleep.
*(She pushes the trolley to the first cell door. Davy opens it. Willie
gathers up his things and moves forward to meet him.)*

Willie Is this me, aye? Released, what?

Davy Sit down, mate. It's only your lunch.

Willie I don't want no lunch. I want out. Out there. *(Whistles)* What
about my soda farls for my mother's tea?

Davy Well, you're not getting out just yet, so you'd better sit down and
eat.

Willie This is out of order. Cat! Rough McFucking Duff, what?

Davy Here, take that.
(Yvonne hands him a plate of food and a cup of tea.)

Willie Thanks, thanks.
(He winks at Yvonne.)
What's your name sweetheart, what's your name? Fancy coming
into my apartment for drinks? *(Laughs)* My apartment! I like, I like, I
like!

Davy Alright, then?

Willie Smashin', smashin'.
(Davy is about to close the door.)
Oh a. . . can I see a smart man, briefcase, briefcase, know a solicitor?

Davy What for?

Willie I wanna make out a will.

Davy What do you want to make out a will for? You're not facing death
just yet.
(Willie scoops up some food on a fork and lets it drop back onto the

12

plate again.)

Willie After I eat this, I will, I will! I'll be dead! *(Whistles)* Jim Reeves! Kaput!
  *(**Davy** closes the door.)*

Yvonne He should feel lucky he's getting anything.

Davy Now, now. Don't be so harsh.

Yvonne Harsh? Rioters and their likes should be burned at the stake.

Davy Your daddy wouldn't like to hear you talk like that.

Yvonne That's why they transferred him to the quieter waters of Donaghadee.

Davy That's no way to be talking about a District Inspector in the RUC.

Yvonne Look, let's have less talk about my father. Open the door.
  *(**Davy** opens **Ambrose**'s door.)*

Davy Lunch.
  *(**Ambrose** gets up and takes the plate and cup. **Davy** closes the door.)*
  Right. Since we're not talking about your father, let's talk about us.

Yvonne There's nothing to say.

Davy I've got two tickets for a concert this Saturday night.

Yvonne I know what your concerts are like.

Davy Do you remember you said you'd like to see your man, you know the guy that hypnotises people?

Yvonne Oh, him. Yeah, I'd love to see him. But I'm washing my hair on Saturday night.

Davy Look, Yvonne. There's no need to give me answers like that. Fair enough, we haven't seen each other in over two weeks, but there's nothing to stop us trying again.

Yvonne I'm not sure, David, I don't know.

Davy You're not going to say we haven't got on well over the past six months.

Yvonne No. It's just that. . . well. . . we don't really have a lot in common, do we?

Davy Not that waffle again.

Yvonne It's not waffle.

Davy All right, so what! You come from the Upper Newtownards Road and I come from the Lower. You live in a big house. I live in a small one. Your father earns twelve thousand a year, mine works in the Shipyard, so frigging what!

Yvonne Keep it down.

Davy *(lowers his voice)* Well, so what?

13

Yvonne *(moving the trolley)* Look, I better get this back, I'm wanted at the desk.

Davy Running away?

Yvonne *(stops)* If you really want an answer – I'm going out with someone.

Davy Who?

Yvonne You wouldn't know him.
(Exits with the trolley.)

Davy *(under his breath)* Bitch!
*(Immediately, loud singing and guitar-playing is heard from **Willie**'s cell. **Davy** makes for the cell door.)*

Willie *(singing)* 'If I got on my knees and I pleaded with you,
 Not to go but to stay in my arms,
 Would you walk out that door
 Like you did once before?
 This time – be different – please stay.'
*(After mixing up the keys, **Davy** finally enters the cell. **Willie** stops singing.)*

Davy What's all the racket about? Where the hell do you think you are, a holiday camp?
(Takes the guitar and throws it on the bed.)

Willie Only singing, only singing!

Davy Well, there'll be no singing in here, right?
(He leaves and locks the door.)

Willie Aye, all right, Quaseemoto!
(Shouting) If this guitar's broke I'm suing you for all you've got! You big girl's blouse, you!
*(**Peter** and **Jackie** are still in the interview room.)*

Peter Stanley's been around a long time. He used to tell me stories about questioning the Republicans in the Fifties. He knew them all. Do you know that at one time there was half-a-dozen men in this Division that could speak fluent Irish?

Jackie It wouldn't be me. I have trouble speaking English.
*(**Stanley** enters the room.)*

Stanley Did you get all the papers, Peter?

Peter Right here, Stanley. *(Lifts a folder and lets it drop.)* Everything you ever wanted to know about Ambrose Fogarty but were afraid to ask.

Stanley Good. You've both read through it?

Jackie Interesting reading.

Peter Not an awful lot of hard evidence, Stanley.

Stanley That's nothing new. The facts are. The bank on the

14

Andersonstown Road was robbed Thursday week ago by three men armed with a machine gun and two pistols. Fogarty was logged by an Army foot patrol an hour before it in Fruithill Park – half a mile away. We have a statement from a regular contact in the Lower Falls, who says. . . Read out the statement, read it out.

Jackie *(reading)* 'I saw Fogarty twice that day. The first time was about half ten in the morning. He seemed to be in a hurry. He got into a red car outside Fusco's chippie on the Grosvenor Road. I couldn't see who the driver of the car was.

'The second time I saw him was at about three o'clock. He drove by me in a white Datsun Estate at the top of Leeson Street. He was driving very fast. Sean McAlister was in the car with him. I never saw him for two days after it.'

Stanley And the bit on the other side.

Jackie 'I heard in the pub that McAlister went across the border because he was involved in robbing a bank or something. I never heard anything about Fogarty except that he's been keeping out of the road.'

Stanley All right. Now. We've three days to get a statement from Fogarty, and quite honestly I don't care how we get it. This man has got away with far too much. I want him charged and parcelled off. I want the pressure piled on. Don't give him a chance to think. Pressure, pressure and more pressure. Any questions?

Jackie Heavy stuff?

Stanley No, no. Go through the usual procedure till we see how it goes.

Peter It should be fun. He's already refused his photo and prints.

Stanley What about that?

Peter I'm expecting it in half an hour.

Stanley Right. Go and get him, Jackie. I'm going to the courthouse. I'll be back shortly.

(Jackie enters the cell area.)

Jackie The prisoner Fogarty please, Davy.

Davy Whatever you say, Jackie.

(Davy sets the clipboard on the table and moves to unlock the door. Jackie lifts the clipboard.)

Jackie Fogarty's eating well, then?

Davy Yep, he ate everything we gave him.

Jackie We'll see if he's still cocky enough to be eating this time tomorrow.

(Jackie sets the clipboard down. Davy opens the cell door.

15

Jackie *steps inside.)*

Jackie Come on with me, Fogarty.

(**Ambrose** *and* **Jackie** *go out towards the interview room.*
Davy *enters the main reception area.)*

Davy They have your man Fogarty away for interview, Sergeant.

Knox It's started, then?

Davy What's he in for, do you know?

Knox Don't know and I don't care. God knows, it's hard enough being a policeman without getting involved in politics.

(**Jackie** *and* **Ambrose** *enter the interview room, where* **Peter** *has been waiting.)*

Jackie Take a seat there.

(**Ambrose** *sits at one side of the table while the two policemen sit on the other. Generally,* **Peter** *asks the questions while* **Jackie** *writes.)*

Peter Right, Ambrose son, just a few questions till we find out a wee bit more about you. Any other first names other than Ambrose?

Ambrose No.

Peter What about nicknames, any nicknames?

Ambrose No.

Peter Tattoos?

Ambrose No.

Peter Any scars or marks anywhere?

Ambrose No.

Peter Address?

Ambrose 202 McDonnell Street.

Peter And your date of birth?

Ambrose 4th of the 11th, '53.

Peter Married?

Ambrose Yes.

Peter Children?

Ambrose Two.

Peter Names.

Ambrose Bronagh and Conor.

Peter Spell 'Bronagh'.

Ambrose B R O N A G H.

Peter Wife's name?

Ambrose Christine.

Peter Wife's maiden name?

16

Ambrose Don't know.

Peter What?

(*Silence*)

You don't know your own wife's maiden name?

Ambrose I'm not answering that question.

Peter Why not?

Ambrose It's got nothing to do with you or me being here.

Peter Is that right? We should have your wife arrested and brought in, then?

(**Ambrose** *shrugs his shoulders.*)

What about brothers and sisters?

Ambrose What about them?

Peter How many have you?

Ambrose I'm not answering that.

Peter You've got an older brother, James; now where does he live?

Ambrose I don't know.

Peter You're a liar.

Jackie Answer the question, Fogarty!

Ambrose I don't know where he lives.

(**Jackie** *throws his pen down and makes to get up.*)

Jackie Right, I'll fuckin' well make you answer.

Peter It's alright, alright.

(**Jackie** *sits down.*)

Ambrose isn't that stupid. He's a bright fella. He knows what's good for him. Give him a minute or two.

(*Silence*)

Now, Ambrose, where does your older brother James live?

Ambrose I don't know.

(**Jackie** *throws his pen down.*)

Peter Why won't you answer?

Ambrose Because my brothers have nothin' to do with me.

Peter Okay, okay. What about sisters? Any married sisters?

Ambrose I'm not answering any more questions about my family.

Jackie What about if we force you to?

Ambrose Force all you want.

(**Jackie** *gets up and stands over* **Ambrose**.)

Jackie C'mere till I tell you, mate. There's bigger men than you's walked in here and walked out with their tails between their legs.

Peter On their way to the hospital wing of Crumlin Road Jail.

Jackie So you better buck up and start answering questions or you'll find yourself in deep trouble very, very soon.

Peter We don't want to go to all that trouble, do we, Ambrose? I mean, we don't want to call in a half-a-dozen soldiers to beat the living daylights out of you, do we? We don't want to have to go and pick up your wife and throw her in one of our cells just to find out her maiden name, now do we?

Jackie By the way, how do you think your wife'll get on without you? Like, when you're locked up in the Kesh for twelve years, do you think she'll find enough things to do about the house? She wouldn't start running to pubs and discos, would she? Neglecting the two kids and everything?

*(**Ambrose** shifts uneasily, agitated.)*

Peter Have you any married sisters, Ambrose?

(Silence)

Well?

Ambrose I'm not answering any more questions about my family.

Peter Fair enough.

*(**Peter** nods to **Jackie**, who leaves the room, and waits outside the door. **Peter** stands up, takes out a packet of cigarettes and comes round to sit on the table beside **Ambrose**. He holds out the packet of cigarettes.)*

Smoke?

*(**Ambrose** looks up at the packet warily, then at **Peter**, then back at the packet. He leans forward and takes a cigarette. **Peter** takes one himself and lights both cigarettes. He draws heavily on the cigarette before casually walking behind **Ambrose**, kicking aimlessly at imaginary objects on the floor.)*

Well, Ambrose, what are we doing with ourselves this weather?

Ambrose Whadaya mean?

Peter I mean, what do you spend your time doing all day?

Ambrose Nothing much.

Peter Do you take a drink?

Ambrose What are you getting at?

Peter Nothing. Listen, Ambrose, I wanna get something clear before we go any further. I'm not trying to trick you into saying something you don't wanna say. I know you're far too shrewd for that oul' game.

Ambrose What am I in here for?

Peter Does it have to be something in particular?

Ambrose You tell me.

Peter It's nothing in particular. Just routine. Wanna cup of tea?

Ambrose That other guy said there was evidence against me about something.

Peter Never listen to him. He just hates people. Do you wanna cup of tea?

Ambrose No.

Peter Are you sure? I can get you one if you want.

Ambrose Na, you're all right, this'll do me. *(Holds up the cigarette.)*

Peter You know, sometimes I get fed up doing this job. I'd love to be able to go to the Ireland match tonight. I always wanted to be a professional footballer anyway. Did you ever play football?

Ambrose Aye.

Peter Much?

Ambrose All my life, up until recently.

Peter Who for?

Ambrose Newsboys Club.

Peter Many's the time I played against them.
(**Ambrose** *looks up, surprised.*)
Remember Boyland? I played for Boyland.

Ambrose What age are you?

Peter That's classified information, but I'll tell you. I was born in 1951.

Ambrose And when did you play for Boyland?

Peter From I was twelve till I was nineteen.

Ambrose Jesus, I musta played against you at some stage.

Peter When were you born, '53? Probably did. God, I used to hate playing against the Newsboys. All wee tough Fenians from York Street, ready to beat you at the drop of a hat.

Ambrose I wasn't from York Street and there was always a couple of Protestants in our team.

Peter I'm sure we played against each other.

Ambrose Nobody'd believe it. Here I am, sitting in a police station, talking to a cop I probably played football against as a teenager? Incredible.

Peter If you'da known then, you'da probably broke my two legs.

Ambrose I was never a dirty player.

Peter Funny the way people pop up after years. I ran into a character the other day, last Tuesday it was, who used to knock about the dances with me in the Sixties. Me and him used to practically live in Romano's.
(**Ambrose** *looks surprised.*)
'Member Romano's?

Ambrose I don't believe this.

Peter What, Romano's in Queen Street? We used to have the wee girls

19

tortured in Romano's. And the Starlight.

Ambrose   Went there, too.

Peter   Betty Staff's, the Jazz Club.

Ambrose   *(laughing)* The Jazz Club! What a place. That used to be the drugs centre then, didn't it? Then they opened the Marquee in Hill Street. I bet you don't remember that one?

Peter   About 1966, '67. I was a real mod by then. Fancied myself as Stevie Marriott outta the Small Faces. Remember the haircuts they all had then? The middle shade, combed back from the crown of the head, all spikey.

Ambrose   That's one thing. I never liked them stupid haircuts. Most of the ones round our way were still only coming round to accepting straight Beatle haircuts. I was always a Rolling Stones man myself. Hair down to there *(demonstrates)* at one stage.

Peter   The Sixties. They were the days. I can honestly say I enjoyed myself then. There was none of the oul' nonsense then, that you get now.

Ambrose   '69 changed all that.

Peter   I remember the night the trouble broke out on the Falls Road. Know where I was? Driving along the Sydenham by-pass with about ten of us packed into my da's car, when it came on the news. I thought I was hearing things. People actually shooting each other in Belfast?

Ambrose   I was supposed to be seeing a wee girl that night, from the Shankill Road would you believe. As soon as I saw the mobs on the road, that was that.

Peter   Little was I to know that two years later I'd be in the RUC Reserve.

Ambrose   With your Stevie Marriott haircut?

Peter   Huh. I'm sure you looked well with your long hair, rioting on the Falls Road.

Ambrose   I did. Funny looking back on it now, but all the rioters in '69 and '70 seemed to be long-haired characters. It musta been a weird sight.

    *(**Peter**, by this time, has casually positioned himself to observe* **Ambrose**.*)*

Peter   What did you do when you got fed up rioting?

    *(***Peter*** is staring shrewdly at* **Ambrose**. **Ambrose** *spots the implications straight away and glances up at* **Peter**, *then looks away.)*

Ambrose   Whadaya mean?

Peter   Listen, Ambrose, I'm not asking anything that the whole world doesn't know. The young long-haired rioters of 1969

20

and '70 became the IRA of '71 and '72. Who doesn't know
that?
(Silence)
You don't have to be ashamed of it.
C'mon, Ambrose, you must have at least, felt, like joining the IRA?

Ambrose   I didn't.

Peter   Never once?

Ambrose   No.

*(**Peter** walks across the room.)*

Peter   Are you afraid in here, Ambrose?

*(**Ambrose** shrugs his shoulders.)*

This isn't Castlereagh, you know.
And for that matter, I'm not so sure that all that much went on in
Castlereagh anyway.
I mean, if you were to believe half the stories.

Ambrose   Am I, am I gonna be beat up in here?

Peter   Why should you?

Ambrose   Why does anybody get beat up? It's an interrogation centre,
isn't it?

Peter   Well, I can put your mind at rest. No, you won't be beaten up. Just
co-operate. That's not much to ask. If you haven't done anything,
you'll walk out, no problem. You scratch our backs and we'll scratch
yours. It's as simple as that.

*(**Peter** opens the door and **Jackie** enters.)*

Jackie   *(harshly)* Let's go Fogarty.

*(**Ambrose** stands up and **Jackie** motions him to the door.)*

Peter   Bring me the other prisoner.
Ambrose?

*(**Ambrose** stops and looks back.)*

Did you ever see the wee girl from the Shankill again?

Ambrose   No.

Peter   Pity.

Ambrose   Was.

*(**Peter** nods in agreement.)*

Peter   I enjoyed the conversation.

*(**Jackie** and **Ambrose** go out to the reception area. **Davy** is chatting to
Knox.)*

Davy   She wouldn't fancy a soldier, would she?

Knox   Maybe he's the 'somebody else' she was talking about.

Jackie   Take this man back to his cell and bring me the other prisoner.

Davy   Right.

(**Davy** *takes* **Ambrose** *to the cells, where he locks him up. He opens* **Willie**'s *door and brings him to* **Jackie**. *During this,* **Jackie** *chats to* **Knox**.)

Jackie   Well, Sergeant, how are things?

Knox   At the moment, alright.

Jackie   Meaning?

Knox   Meaning, I don't expect things to remain in order in this police station over the next seventy-two hours.

Jackie   Ah, you're a worrier.

Knox   I'm also a policeman.

Jackie   What do you think I am, a fuckin' traffic warden? I've a job to do. If you happen to bear the brunt of complaints, that's hard luck.

Knox   If there are any complaints from any of these prisoners, I have my duty to carry out.

Jackie   You just do that, Sergeant. If I can be of any assistance?

   (**Davy** *and* **Willie** *enter.*)

Davy   Prisoner Lagan.

Jackie   What? This is the man involved in the rioting? You're a brave hairy-arsed Fianna boy. C'mon with me.

   (**Jackie** *and* **Willie** *go to the interview room.*)

Knox   Now, if they molest an unfortunate fella like that, they're capable of anything.

Peter   *(in the interview room)* The boul' Willie Lagan. Take a seat there, Willie.

   (**Jackie** *and* **Willie** *sit down.*)

   Well, Willie, what's all this about you leading the rioters on the Falls Road?

   (**Willie** *sits in silence.*)

   Well?

   Willie, I am speaking to you.

   (**Willie** *turns his head away.*)

   What's wrong, have you lost your tongue? Willie! If there's something wrong, why don't you tell us what it is.

   Why aren't you talking?

Willie   *(abruptly)* I'm on hunger-strike.

   (**Jackie** *and* **Peter** *look at each other, in humorous disbelief.*)

Peter   What? Did you say hunger-strike?

Willie   Until death! The lot! No food, no water, nothing!

Peter   You must be joking.

Willie   I'll be a martyr, a martyr in a fortnight. *(Whistles)* Finito!

Peter   Willie, all that we want is for you to tell us what happened that made the soldiers arrest you?

Willie Big funeral, thousands, tricolour, tricolour over the top of my coffin. Hunger-strike, that's it, that's it!

Peter Willie, I'm going to ask you one question and I want an answer, or else. Did you or did you not throw bottles at the Army?

Willie Hunger-strike, hunger-strike.

*(**Jackie** stands up and places himself behind **Willie**.)*

Peter Are you still not answering any questions?

*(**Willie** doesn't reply. **Peter** nods and **Jackie** slaps **Willie** on the back of the head.)*

Willie Which particular question was it, which one?

Peter That's better. Here.

*(Hands **Willie** a pen and paper.)*

Write down on that, everything that happened. Why you threw the bottles at the Army. And sign it at the bottom.

*(**Willie** laughs, roars and whistles.)*

Willie I like, I like, I like.

*(He beckons **Peter** to shake hands with him.)*

Smart, smart. Bamber Gasgoigne. I like, I like, I like. Sign a statement!

Peter Take him back to his cell.

Willie What, what, what! I want out.

Peter Back to his cell.

*(**Jackie** stands **Willie** up.)*

Willie I wanna see a man with a briefcase, know, a shirt-and-tie job.

Peter You'll see a solicitor soon enough. Tell the Desk Sergeant to have his questioning handled by someone else. Tell him to give McMinn a buzz.

Jackie Right. Come on you.

Willie Here, listen. What about my ma's tea, like?

Peter What about your mother's tea?

Willie I have the soda farls for her tea in my cell. What'll I do, what?

Jackie Come on.

*(**Willie** shouts and protests as he is led out.)*

Knox *(on radio)* Return to base, Eight One, and pick up a new crew member, over.

Radio Roger, out.

*(**Jackie** and **Willie** enter.)*

Jackie Prisoner for the cells.

Davy Right.

*(**Davy** exits with **Willie**.)*

Jackie Sergeant, you're requested to have Lagan's questioning handled by somebody else. He said, try McMinn.

Knox Will do.

Jackie And we didn't get a copy of the arresting soldier's statement.

Knox I thought that was sent through.

Jackie We never got it.

Knox Yvonne? Yvonne?

Yvonne *(entering)* Sergeant?

Knox What has happened that statement of the arresting soldier, in reference to the Lagan charge?

Yvonne Sent up five minutes ago, Sergeant.

Jackie Thanks. Better late than never. See that McMinn gets it, Sergeant, will you?
(Exits.)

Yvonne What's wrong with him?

Knox Absolutely nothing. Civility is not included in the training of that lot.

Yvonne *(turning to go)* Doesn't seem like it.
Have you seen that Captain about, Sergeant?

Knox Captain?

Yvonne You know, the arresting soldier?

Knox Oh, no, no. That's another one. The less I see of him the better. I'd say he's probably back out on the front line. The rioters burned a bus a while back.
*(**Davy** enters.)*
Was it important?

Yvonne Nothing that can't wait.
*(She looks at **Davy** and goes out.)*

Davy Sergeant, that man's a lunatic. He's ranting on about Bamber Gascoigne going on hunger-strike or something.

Knox That poor fella probably doesn't know whether he's coming or going.

Davy But he's a geg, isn't he? Always telling jokes. Hear the one he told me?
Two Irishmen having a row. One says, 'I'm the biggest liar in the world.'
The other one says, 'No, you're not, I am.'
The first fella says, 'Prove it.'
Your man thinks for a moment and then says, 'I've swam up the Niagara Falls.'
The other fella says, 'That's nothing, I saw you doing it.'

24

(Knox and Davy laugh. Davy leans forward on the desk, looks about him, and speaks almost in a whisper.)

Davy Sergeant. Do you believe that the Special Branch really. . .

Knox CID, Davy. CID is the official term, remember.

Davy Well, do they actually beat people up? Like, I mean, is everything you hear about them true?

Knox What have you heard?

Davy Bits and pieces here and there.

Knox Good or bad?

Davy Both, really.

Knox Let me ask you something, Davy. How long are you out of Enniskillen?

Davy Six, twelve, eighteen months. One year in Dromara and the rest here.

Knox How long have you been doing cell duties?

Davy About a month.

Knox Come back to me in six months and we'll have a long chat about it, if you want.

Davy But if there's so much. . .

Knox Not now.

Davy Yes, okay. Oh, ah, Sergeant? You couldn't tell me what duties Yvonne's on next week?

Knox I thought you'd packed that in.

Davy I was just wondering would we be on the same shift. I'll have to get talking to her.

Knox You must have the bug very bad, Davy.

Davy I wouldn't go as far as to say that.

*(**Knox** checks a ledger.)*

Knox As it happens, you should just about bump into each other here and there.

Davy Sound, sound.

Knox Try and be a wee bit more discreet, Constable McFadden, would you, please?

*(A loud yell is heard from **Willie**'s cell.)*

Davy What's that?

Knox Sounds like your friend.

Davy I wonder what to hell's wrong now.

*(**Davy** hurries to **Willie**'s cell. As he opens the cell door, **Willie** falls out onto the floor beside him and lies motionless. When **Davy** leans over to pick him up, **Willie** makes a botched attempt to snatch the keys. **Davy** quickly gets him to his feet, twisting **Willie**'s arm up his*

25

back. **Davy** *speaks angrily.)*
What in the name of heaven are you playing at?
Willie　It always works for George Raft. *(Laughs.)*
　　*(***Davy** *locks* **Willie** *back in his cell as* **Jackie** *arrives.)*
Jackie　Prisoner Fogarty, please, Davy?
Davy　Right.
　　*(***Davy** *opens* **Ambrose**'s *cell door.* **Jackie** *steps inside.)*
Jackie　On your feet, Fogarty.
　　*(***Ambrose** *stands up.* **Jackie** *waves a chit of paper.)*
Fingerprints and photographs, Fogarty.
　　(He moves closer, waving the chit at **Ambrose**'s *face.)*
Specially signed just for you, Mr Know-all.
　　(Black-out.)

Act Two

Yvonne *is busy on the radio. The prisoners are eating.*

Yvonne   If you would go to that location, Two One, and check with the
lady in the house, over.
Radio   It's definitely a B and E?
Yvonne   Yes. Entry was gained through the back door. The meter's been
robbed and some items taken from a jewellery box. She only
discovered it this morning and apparently she's very upset.
Radio   We'll go there now, out.
(**Ambrose** *is eating in his cell.*)
Ambrose   I must say, I find nothing wrong with the food. But then again,
as my mother used to say when I was a kid, *(mimics)* 'Our Ambrose
doesn't eat to live, he lives to eat.' My da put it more bluntly, 'Our
Ambrose? He'd eat shite only for the smell of it.'
(**Ambrose** *is enjoying his food. He feels good and is obviously
amused at his current thoughts. He finishes his meal and stands up.*)
I don't feel too bad, not bad at all. If the next forty-eight hours is like
the last twenty-four. . .
(Sings)
'Baby – everything is all right, uptight.
Way outta sight, yeah.
Baby. . .'
What'll I do now? Have to work out something to keep the mind
occupied.
A pen? A pen would come in handy. Write my life story on these
walls.
This is Monday, isn't it? I wonder did Christine get Conor to school.
Probably didn't. It's at times like these that the wee bugger plays her
up. Anytime I'm away.
I wonder has she. . . I'm sure she's been ringing up about me. A
solicitor.
I wonder when they're gonna interview me again. What in the name

27

of Jesus could it be?

Probably try and bluff me into signing a statement about something or other. Probably go straight for my balls. I'll probably sign.

(*Laughs*)

Squeal on everybody.

(*Mimics*)

'I wasn't me, Mister, it was Billy O'Neill. I only got a lift in the car.' Right. Exercises. I'll have a walt at doing some exercises. Keep me on the go. Press-ups. Try some press-ups.

(*He gets down on the floor and starts doing press-ups. Sings*)

'Jump down, turn around, pick a bale of cotton.

Jump down, turn around, pick a bale of hay.'

(*Continues singing.*

The **Captain** *enters the main reception area.*)

Captain   Just the girl I'm looking for.

Yvonne   What do you want now?

Captain   Nothing personal, it's nothing personal.

(*He stands to attention and salutes.*)

My commanding officer requests a copy of the statement by the arresting soldier, Captain Levington, in relation to the arrest of the prisoner Lagan – Sir!

Yvonne   There are only two and they're in use at the moment.

Captain   Would it be too much to ask that the police photocopy one more and have it sent through to Major Higginbottom?

Yvonne   I'll see about it.

Captain   And while we're on the subject of requests, Yvonne, would you care to join me at the stock-car racing this weekend?

Yvonne   Stock-car racing?

Captain   Don't think I haven't heard all about you.

Yvonne   Where did you hear that?

Captain   Now, now, a copper wouldn't ask that.

Yvonne   You don't waste much time.

Captain   We're only on this earth the once. Well? Are we going to the stock-car racing? Ballymena or some place?

Yvonne   We have done our homework.

Captain   (*mimics Belfast accent*) I was talking to a few peelers like, know what I mean?

Yvonne   (*sarcastically*) Ha, ha.

Captain   Well?

Yvonne   I'll think about it.

Radio Bravo Hotel, Bravo Hotel from One One, over.

Yvonne Send, over.

Radio Returning to base to drop one crew member, over.

Yvonne Roger on that.

Captain Wait a minute! Who is it, who does that voice remind me of? Quick, quick. . . yes, got it. Faye Dunaway. If I didn't know, Yvonne, I would swear blind that I was standing here listening to Faye Dunaway.

Yvonne Do you chat up all the girls like this?

Captain Only the ones I fancy. Now, what do you say? Are we going to the stock-car racing or are we not?

Yvonne I told you. I'll have to think about it.

Captain What is there to think about?

Yvonne I hardly know you, for a start.

Captain And how are you supposed to get to know me?

Yvonne I told you, I'll think about it.

(Davy enters.)

Captain Oh, here's the RUC's answer to Lieutenant Theo Kojak. How's it going, Theo?

(Davy ignores the Captain.)

Davy I think the prisoners have finished their lunch, Yvonne.

Yvonne It'll have to wait a few minutes till Sergeant Knox comes back.

Captain Why don't you clear up the dirty plates, Theo? A supercop can do anything. *(Laughs.)*

Davy Have I done something on you, Captain?

Captain Oh-oh. Kojak's annoyed. Better go before I get arrested. See ya, Yvonne!

Yvonne Bye, Captain!

(The Captain turns to Davy.)

Captain Listen, Crocker, I've only got twenty-four hours in the day. I want every suspect on the Lower East Side in this building by ten o'clock.

(As he goes) Who loves ya, baby!

Yvonne I don't think you like Colin?

Davy Oh, we're on first-name terms are we?

Yvonne I heard it somewhere.

Davy And you're right, I don't particularly like him.

Yvonne Why not? I think he's very attractive. He's funny to talk to.

Davy If that's what you're looking for, why don't you go out with Billy Connolly?

Yvonne Nasty, nasty.

29

Davy   Yeah. Did you get the message your father left?

Yvonne   He was here?

Davy   No, I was with him this morning. He told me to tell you your sister's coming back from Rhodesia in a fortnight's time.

Yvonne   Sandra! That's great. That's really great. Where was Dad?

Davy   At 'C' Division. He, ah. . . he wants me to come out to your house at the weekend to finish the trench.

Yvonne   Oh. I thought he'd got somebody else to do that.

Davy   He couldn't. He said I started it so I may as well finish it. You'll be off at the weekend?

Yvonne   Yeah, I'm going to the stock-car racing at Ballymena.

Davy   ⎫ *(simultaneously)*   Who with?
Yvonne   ⎬   With a friend!

Yvonne   I told you I was seeing someone else.

Davy   You helped me to start the trench.

Yvonne   I won't be helping you to finish it.

(Knox enters.)

Oh, Sergeant. Inspector Wright wants you to phone him and there's a message from Community Relations.

Knox   Thanks, Yvonne.

(He lifts the telephone receiver.)

Have you nothing to do, Mr McFadden?

(Peter and Jackie enter the interview room.)

Jackie   I've no doubt that, only for m'da, I'd be in the UDA the day.

Peter   He stopped you?

Jackie   Well, he made me realise that going down to Unity Flats and throwing bricks through people's windows wasn't really a devastating blow to the IRA.

I was just counting up the other day. Out of our class at school, there's two dead, fourteen in the UDA, four in the UVF, three UDR and only one peeler. Fuckin' me.

Peter   There's seven of my classmates in the RUC and another two in the UDR. I don't think anybody joined the paramilitaries. There was one fella, Burrows. He robbed my father's shop and claimed the money was for the UVF. Turned out, it was to buy a blue second-hand Toyota to drive his bird about in.

Jackie   Bangor's a wee bit quieter than the Shankill Road though, isn't it?

Peter   Except when a crowd of soldiers get a lot of firewater in them.

Jackie   Yeah, going round chasin' all your women. The Brits used to drink on our road a lot but after a foot patrol shot dead a couple of men in a bar, it all stopped.

30

Do you remember that time?

Peter   Vaguely.

Jackie   Vaguely! Shows you, doesn't it. If you die in ones and twos here now, nobody remembers you. It has to be McGurk's Bar or Warrenpoint before it rings a bell, even six months later.

(Stanley enters.)

Stanley   How are we getting on, alright?

Peter   Just waiting on you.

Stanley   Right, the report is that McAlister, who was in the car with Fogarty that day, is definitely across the border, living in Dublin. That'll be a good area to push Fogarty on. Try and shake his confidence. Is he still eating?

Peter   Never leaves a scrap. Rapped the cell door last night and asked for more chips. Wanted another cup of tea this morning.

Stanley   No loss of appetite. Is he sleeping?

Peter   He has been sleeping well, too.

Stanley   Well, we'll see what effect the next couple of interviews have on him. What time was that first interview at yesterday?

Peter   Two-thirty p.m.

Stanley   So it's nearly twenty-four hours since his last questioning.

Peter   Twenty hours and sixteen minutes, to be precise.

Stanley   He'll be dying to talk.

Peter   I've a feeling the volcano'll bubble over today. It's a long time to be on your own.

Stanley   But it's getting him to talk about the right things. Get him in, Jackie.

*(**Jackie** goes to the cells.)*

Peter   It should be interesting to hear his excuse for being in Fruithill Park an hour before the robbery.

What do you think?

Stanley   Cutting some oul' woman's grass or something, I suppose.

Peter   No, I mean, what do you think of Fogarty?

Stanley   He's a bastard.

Peter   Is he active in military operations?

Stanley   Of course he is. What the hell do you think I have him in for?

Peter   But, looking at his record, it's a series of contacts and informants saying that they think he's a Quartermaster, they heard he was OC, he was seen with such and such.

The only thing we can say for sure is that he's active politically. He is seen with men we know are operators, and must know a certain amount about them.

Stanley Ambrose Fogarty is in the IRA. He's active militarily, and if you read that report again, you'll see that he was actually seen with a rifle in 1973. All those reports can't be wrong. One or two, yes, but not seventeen of them, going back nearly ten years.
He is in the IRA. But he's one of the clever sort. Thinks he is anyway. I'm sure he knows plenty about this robbery.
*(**Jackie** enters.)*

Jackie Want him in?
*(**Stanley** nods. **Jackie** opens the door wide and **Ambrose** enters.*
Jackie exits.)*

Peter Sit down, Ambrose.
*(**Ambrose** sits.)*
Been getting enough to eat?
*(**Ambrose** shrugs. **Peter** refers to a file.)*
Ambrose Fogarty! Public Enemy Number One. You know why you're here, don't you?

Ambrose Nobody's told me anything.

Peter Where were you Thursday week ago?

Ambrose When was that?

Peter Not last Thursday but the Thursday before, of course.

Ambrose Am. . . Thursday. . . week ago. . . I. . . a. . . I'm not sure. . . a. . .

Peter You work, don't you?

Ambrose No.

Peter On the dole?

Ambrose Aye.

Peter And you can't remember the Thursday I'm talking about? Thursday the 6th.

Ambrose It's difficult. I'm not sure if. . .

Stanley Refresh his memory.

Peter It was the day you were driving about in a white Datsun car with Sean McAlister.

Ambrose Yes. Yes, I remember that.

Peter What were you doing with him?

Ambrose I was helping him to do a wee bit of work repairing a pub downtown.

Peter Which pub?

Ambrose A pub in an entry off Ann Street. I don't know the name of it.

Peter Which entry?

Ambrose There's two or three entries off Ann Street. I'm not sure which one it was, honest.

Peter Okay. So what time did you start work at this pub and what time did you finish?

Ambrose Look, what is all this about?

Peter Just answer the question.

Ambrose Am. . . started around eleven. We worked till about one or so and then we knocked off.

Stanley Very convenient.

Peter What did you do then?

Ambrose Went to a pub.

Peter Which one?

Ambrose The White Fort.

Peter On the Andersonstown Road? What did you go away up there for?

Ambrose We had another job to do in the afternoon, so Sean suggested the White Fort 'cause it was near the place we were going to.

Stanley What position does Sean McAlister hold in your unit?

Ambrose What?

Stanley Answer the question.

Ambrose I'm not in any unit.

Stanley You're a liar!

Peter Where was this job you had to do?

Ambrose Off Fruithill Park. . . Glenhill Park, that's it.

Peter What was the job?

Ambrose Repairing a roof.

Peter What was the number of the house?

Ambrose No idea.

Stanley Just hold on a minute. What do you think we are, fools? You don't know the name of the pub. You don't know what entry it was in and now you say you don't know the number of the house that you fixed a roof on?

Ambrose I don't remember them sort of details.

Stanley *(shouting)* You better start remembering!

Ambrose I didn't take any interest in the places. Sean did that. They were his jobs.

Peter What do you mean?

Ambrose The work belonged to Sean and his brother. I was only there one day because his Joe was sick and couldn't weigh in. I'm sure Sean knows all the addresses.

Peter Do you think we should pull McAlister in then?

Ambrose 'S up to you.

Stanley What do you mean, 'It's up to you,' and you sitting there knowing fine rightly the bastard's across the border!

Ambrose Only for two weeks.

Stanley What do you mean, 'Only for two weeks'?

Ambrose Him and his Joe's away working in Dublin on a job for two weeks. He'll be back up this weekend as far as I know.

Peter Tell us this, Ambrose. Were you walking along Fruithill Park at any time that day?

Ambrose Aye. . . we parked the car outside the house we were working at and walked down to the pub.

Peter Walked?

Ambrose Sean said he didn't want to go down in the car. He wanted to walk.

Stanley You're lying through your teeth! You mean you had a car and you decided to walk instead.

Stanley ⎫ *(simultaneously)* You expect us to believe that!
Ambrose ⎭ He said he was fed up driving.

Stanley Eh?

Ambrose Sean said he was fed up driving.

(Stanley gets up and moves round to shout into Ambrose's face.)

Stanley Fed up nothing! He wasn't fed up when you and him robbed the bank on the Andersonstown Road, was he?

Ambrose What?

Stanley Yes, sonny. Don't put on your big innocent face in here. Instead of so-called working at a roof, you two reprobates spent the early part of the afternoon planning to commit a crime.

Ambrose You must be joking.

Stanley Shut up! And only speak when you're spoken to, right? You're not walking out of here this time, Fogarty. The two of you robbed that bank and McAlister's took himself off, leaving you to take the rap!

(He walks around behind Ambrose.)

That's comrades for you! You can be sure he's laughing his head off at oul' stupid Fogarty right now. Pinting it in some pub in Dublin. Now, before we waste any more time, you *(shoves a pen and paper in front of Ambrose)* write down there your involvement in this whole thing and let's have less of the oul' nonsense. I've had enough of you!

(Silence. Ambrose looks down at his hands.)

Peter Well, Ambrose?

Stanley Start writing.

Ambrose   I wasn't involved in anything.

Stanley   I said, start writing!

(**Stanley** *grabs* **Ambrose** *by the shoulder of the coat and shakes him.*)

Do you not hear or what, sonny? Lift that pen!

(*He lifts the pen and places it between* **Ambrose**'s *fingers.*)

Start writing, kid!

(*Silence.*

Ambrose *lets the pen fall from his hand.*

Stanley *grabs* **Ambrose's** *jaw and turns his face round to within an inch of his own.*)

I'm telling you for the last bloody time. Pick that pen up and write! We know you were there.

(*Stanley steps back.*

Ambrose *stares down blankly.*)

Peter   Ambrose, what time did you say you finished working on the roof at?

Ambrose   Around four.

Peter   Around four. And what?

Ambrose   Went home.

Peter   Didn't go to the pub?

Ambrose   Straight home.

Peter   With McAlister?

(**Ambrose** *nods.*)

Stanley   Where did you count the money?

Ambrose   There was no money.

Stanley   How much did you cop for yourself?

Ambrose   There was no money.

Stanley   Liar! You're a liar, Fogarty. And believe you me, we'll cut the lying out of you over the next two days.

Peter   Whereas, if you sign a statement, Ambrose, everything'll be so much easier for you.

(*Silence*)

Okay. Let me put it this way. Maybe you just drove the car or did lookout. We've a fair idea it was McAlister and a few others who actually robbed the bank. All we want is for you to write down about McAlister. Tell us the names of the others involved.

Right, so you did lookout or some other minor role. We can have a talk with the judge about that. Two-year suspended sentence. No more. Eh?

Ambrose   I wasn't involved in anything.

(**Stanley** *gives* **Peter** *the nod.*

Peter *stands up.)*

Peter It's up to yourself, Ambrose lad. You can have it the easy way or the hard way. We're only doing a job. We want it the easy way. Think about it, what? C'mon with me.

*(**Ambrose** stands up.)*

Stanley Let me tell you something, Fogarty. We have three signed statements from three of your mates confirming your membership. So no matter what way it goes, you're getting done.

If we do you on the main charge of armed robbery you'll get anything up to fourteen years. Taken in possession, intent and so on.

Or we could do you with membership. That's anything up to seven years.

Maybe even both.

Peter Or, as I said, you could sign for a minor part in the robbery. The judge can throw all the blame on McAlister, who's across the border, we'll drop the membership thing and you'll walk away with an eighteen-month suspended under your arm. Couldn't be simpler. Anyway, we'll get you back to your cell so that you can have a nice long rest.

Stanley To think everything over carefully.

Peter Only another two full days to go.

*(**Peter** opens the door, beckons **Ambrose** out and leaves with him. **Willie** starts banging on his cell door. **Davy** opens it.)*

Davy What's the problem here?

Willie Quick, quick! What time is it? Time?

Davy It's wearing round to tea time.

Willie Not long to go, not long to go. Here, *(holds out his parcel)* take these farls down to 95 Grosvenor Place and tell my mother I'm sorry, I'll be home late.

Davy What?

Willie Quick. They're for my ma's tea. Quick, not long to go, not long to go.

Davy I thought they were for the tea yesterday?

Willie Doesn't matter, doesn't matter, she mightn't've noticed. Quick, quick.

Davy Catch yourself on, mate.

Tell me this. Why do you say everything twice?

Willie Whadaya mean, whadaya mean?

Davy You just done it.

Willie What? You trying to make fun outta me, what? I'll smack you, smack you. *(Poses)* I'll drop you like a ton of bricks, ton of bricks.

36

Wanna use the toilet, quick piss, quick piss, know.

Davy Oh, c'mon.

(Just as **Willie** *leaves his cell,* **Ambrose** *arrives, escorted by* **Peter**.*)*

Peter Prisoner for you.

Willie Ambrose! Ambrose! What about you, our kid, alright, alright?

Ambrose Hi, Willie.

Davy That's enough, back in.

Willie You arrested, arrested?

Davy I said back inside. Back inside.

(He pushes **Willie** *back into his cell and locks the door.)*

Right.

(To **Ambrose**.*)* In you go.

*(**Ambrose** is locked up while* **Peter** *leaves.*

Willie *starts banging on his cell door again.* **Davy** *opens it.)*

Davy All right, I'm coming, I'm coming!

Willie That's twice you said that, twice.

(Laughs.)

Go for a piss nigh, go nigh?

Davy C'mon

*(**Davy** leaves with* **Willie**. **Knox** *and* **Yvonne** *are at the reception desk.)*

Knox And you feel under pressure from your father to stay on?

Yvonne Sort of. Let's put it this way. He doesn't tell me I have to stay on, in fact we don't even talk about it, but I know if I left the force he'd be very, very disappointed.

Knox That's a kind of pressure.

Yvonne But I really want to travel while I'm still young. America, Canada, Egypt, anywhere really. What is there here? This place'll never sort itself out. You'd have more fun living on a desert island with Malcolm Muggeridge than carrying on in this place. At least, not while the IRA's allowed to do what it wants. I want out. Fast.

Knox Then get out. I've no doubt your father will understand.

Yvonne You obviously don't know him well enough. My father just lives for this job.

His father before him was an RIC man all his life in County Monaghan. I have no brothers, so it's me that's expected to carry on the tradition.

Knox If your heart's not in it. . .

Yvonne I can't just get up and go.

Knox Why not? Yvonne, let me give you a word of advice. My mother, God have mercy on her, lived till she was ninety-two and never saw further than the Castlereagh Hills.

You're what, twenty-two, twenty-three? Get away out of this and have a look around you while you have nothing to tie you down. Go and see how the rest of the world lives. There's over one hundred and fifty countries and as many languages, religions and traditions. But don't – whatever you do – don't spend the rest of your life regretting that you didn't do it. And don't stay at this game – especially if your heart's not in it.

Yvonne Is yours?

Knox Yeah, strangely enough it is. I'm a bit like your father. I actually like the job.

Yvonne But do you not get disheartened when you don't see yourself getting anywhere? No end to the Troubles? You've been at this station, I don't know how long, and the people outside that front gate still resent you.

Knox That's probably the thing that gets me most. I'd love to walk out there one day on my own. Dander up the road a bit and some wee woman come up to me and say, 'Good morning, Sergeant Knox,' or some such trivial greeting. That would mean a lot to me.

Yvonne As it is, you're more likely to get your head blown off.

Knox Many's a man I knew well. You know, everytime word comes in of one of the lads being shot dead or blown up, I experience it all myself. I feel the pain, see the blood and can't help but harbour the bitterness. And I feel the fear. Every single time. The fear that it might be Sergeant Trevor Knox, number 15537, the next time around.

Yvonne When I get to America I'll send you an application form for the New York Police Department.

Knox No thanks. I joined long before the Troubles started, there's no point in leaving now. I'm a policeman. Belfast, Birmingham or Baltimore. That's it. Just get on with your job. Nothing else for it.

Radio Bravo Whisky Nine One to Bravo Hotel. Bravo Whisky Nine One to Bravo Hotel, over.

Yvonne Well, you can count me out.

(She moves over and answers the radio.)

Nine One, send over.

*(**Knox** laughs and returns to some paperwork.)*

Radio Permission to contact Alfa Romeo, over.

Yvonne Go ahead, Nine One, over.

*(**Willie** and **Davy** enter.)*

Willie Sure that's nothing, they've decided to build a swimming pool round our way. The Committee came to my door last week collecting for it.

Davy   And did you give them anything?

Willie   Aye, a bucket of water!

*(**Davy** and **Willie** laugh as **Willie** is locked up.)*

Ambrose   *(walking in a figure-of-eight round his cell)* '62 winners were Tottenham. Team was Brown, Baker, Henry, Norman. . . No, Brown, Baker, Henry, *Blanchflower*, Norman. McKay, Medwin, White, Greaves – no, Jimmy Greaves wasn't in that team. Smith, Allen, I think, and Cliff Jones. I wonder was Dyson there? '63 winners were Manchester United. Team was, Gaskill, Dunne, Brennan – no, I wonder was that that team. . . Hold on. . . Frig it. . . I don't know. I'll come back to that. . .

Back to Heavyweights. Where was I. . . 1929. . . Jack Dempsey versus Gene Tunney. . .

(Sings)

'Now he's gonna fight Jack Dempsey

That was me brother Silvest. . .'

Tunney beat Dempsey, right. That was the famous 'long count' fight. Tunney retired undefeated. Then there was Irishman James J. Braddock. . .

(Stops)

I definitely reckon the last interview went okay. At least nobody got really violent. Maybe your man was right. Maybe I won't be beat up. I'd hate to have the back of my hair pulled.

(He stretches his hand up and tugs at the front of his hair. He then does the same with the hair at the lower back of his head. He immediately winces.)

I don't think I could take too much of that. Torture, starvation, brutality, yes, but leave the back of my hair alone, please.

'Excuse me, you wouldn't start pulling out my finger nails one by one and leave the back of my hair alone?'

I'll never forget the Christian Brother. Gibbons his name was. Trailed me out to the front of the class regularly, by the back of the hair. Tears welled in my eyes, but there was no way I was gonna make a sound in front of the rest of the class.

(Laughs)

Not like Dominic O'Reilly. Or Phoenix.

Ach, what am I talking about, I'm still alive. I think it's gonna be all right. I think I can manage. I'm sure it's all in the mind. I think I can afford a lie-down.

(He moves down onto the bed.)

Now, who took the title off Braddock? Max Baer, yes, Max Baer, around 19. . . 34. . .

(Stanley and Peter enter the interview room.)

Stanley The next two days are crucial, Peter. I want you to make sure this fella's kept in complete isolation. No cellmates, no newspapers, no news, no conversation whatsoever outside this room. I don't want him to know what time of the day or night it is.

Peter But those are all standard regulations.

Stanley I know that, but I want you to check that they're being carried out to the letter. I want this man.

(Jackie enters the cell area and collects Ambrose.)

After this interview, I want to check out his story. Find out which bar off Ann Street has had repairs carried out. Get somebody to have a look at every single roof in Glenhill Park, and find out if any work's been done there. And, just on the off-chance, check on the McAlisters. See what the family says about the two brothers going to Dublin. One good break's all we need, and this fella's story'll collapse around his ears.

(Jackie pushes open the interview room door and enters with Ambrose.)

Peter I'm beginning to agree with you. I think it's one big cock-and-bull story.

Stanley You better believe it. Right, I'll leave you two to it. I'll be about. *(Exit.)*

Peter Ambrose! My oul' son. How's the world treating you, eh? Take a wee seat there.

(Ambrose sits. Peter turns to Jackie)

Did you hear about Ambrose's last interview?

Jackie No, what?

Peter He sat and spun us a load of lies.

Jackie Did he?

Peter I nearly busted out laughing a couple of times, it was that funny.

Jackie A bit of a comedian, is he?

Peter Hysterical.

(Jackie takes off his coat and rolls up his sleeves.)

Jackie Well, we'll soon see if he knows any new jokes, 'cause I'm not in the form to listen to jokes *(leans into Ambrose's face)* from anybody! Especially from a no-good bank-robber! A thief!

(Jackie stands behind Ambrose.)

Peter Right, Ambrose, from the start. Tell me everything you did on Thursday the 6th.

Ambrose Again?

40

Peter   Again. Word for word.

Jackie   And every time you tell a lie, I'm gonna knock your bollocks in. Have you got that?

*(***Ambrose*** looks at **Jackie**, then stares straight in front.)*

Peter   Go ahead, Ambrose. From the moment you got up.

Ambrose   I've already told yiz.

Peter   We forget. So tell us again.

Ambrose   I was working that day with Sean McAlister.

Jackie   Operations Officer in the Lower Falls.

Ambrose   We did a job in a pub and. . .

Peter   What time did you start at?

Ambrose   About eleven o'clock, but. . .

Jackie   Where was the pub?

Ambrose   Off Ann Street. I told. . .

Jackie   What was the name of it, and if you say you don't know I'm gonna punch you.

(Silence)

Ambrose   I don't know.

*(***Jackie*** slaps **Ambrose**'s face.)*

Peter   What work did you do in this pub?

Ambrose   *(agitated)* Plastered the walls in the toilets.

Peter   I didn't know you were a plasterer.

Ambrose   I'm not. I just laboured to Sean.

Peter   Then what?

Ambrose   Went to a pub.

Peter   What time did you finish work in the pub?

Ambrose   About one.

Peter   And you went to another pub round the corner?

Ambrose   No, on the Andersonstown Road. The White Fort.

Jackie   What to fuck were you doing up there?

Ambrose   Having a drink before our next job.

Jackie   The bank?

Ambrose   Repairing a roof.

Jackie   Where?

Ambrose   Glenhill Park, off Fruithill.

Jackie   That's the street facing St Teresa's Chapel?

Ambrose   Aye. It's. . .

Jackie   Which house?

Ambrose   I'm not sure of the number.

Peter   *(mimics)* He's not sure of the number.

Jackie   What about the name of the family?

Peter Are you joking? The way Ambrose has this story worked out, it doesn't allow for names of streets, or pubs, or numbers of houses, and definitely not names of families.

Jackie What was the name of the family?

Ambrose I don't know.

Peter Ambrose, do you have a permanently bad memory?

Ambrose No, I just remember the things I'm interested in.

Peter What time did you finish there at?

Ambrose I think it was about three.

Peter Is that right?

Ambrose Yeah, about three.

Peter You're definite about that?

Ambrose I couldn't tell you the exact time, but I think it was around three.

Jackie That proves it, doesn't it?

Ambrose Proves what?

Jackie Proves that everything that comes out of your mouth is lies. Because fifteen minutes ago you told us you finished work at four o'clock. Now you're saying three. Which is it, lad?

Peter Was it three or four, Ambrose?

Jackie You'd better make up your mind. If you're gonna tell lies, at least stick to the same lie!

Ambrose I'm not telling any lies.

Jackie What's that then, a slip of the tongue?

Ambrose It's nearly two weeks ago. As far as I can remember we finished about three o'clock.

(Peter stands up.)

Peter Ambrose, stand up.

(Ambrose looks uncertain.)

I said, on your feet.

(Ambrose stands up.)

Move out to the middle of the room.

(Ambrose takes a few steps.)

Hands down straight by your side.

(Ambrose responds.)

Did you say you were married?

Ambrose Yes.

Peter Does your wife enjoy it?

Jackie *(laughing)* Enjoy it? That dying-looking bastard couldn't satisfy our budgie.

Peter Is that right, Ambrose?

42

Ambrose What?

Peter Can you not satisfy your wife?

(**Ambrose** *remains silent.*)

Jackie Listen, mate, you've just been asked a question, would you like to answer it?

(*Silence*)

Peter He'd probably tell us a pack of lies anyway.

Jackie I bet you his willie's not the size of my wee finger.

Peter Is that right, Ambrose? Is that right? Answer me.

Ambrose I'm not answering any personal question.

(*Silence*)

Peter Take off your clothes.

(**Ambrose** *looks at him sharply. He stares disbelievingly.*)

Everything. Take off all your clothes, Ambrose.

Jackie (*laughing*) This should be fun. I should've brought my telescope with me.

Peter Take off his coat for him.

(**Jackie** *roughly takes* **Ambrose**'s *coat off him.*)

Now, Ambrose, I believe in democracy, I'm giving you the choice of taking your own clothes off, or he takes them off for you.

Ambrose You must be joking.

Peter Do you think so? Take off his shoes.

(**Jackie** *takes off* **Ambrose**'s *shoes.*)

Now, to get to the point. Are you gonna sign a statement about the robbery, or do we strip you naked and leave you standing here for a couple of hours?

Ambrose I can't tell you anything about any robbery, 'cause I didn't do anything.

Peter Membership?

Ambrose I'm not a member of anything.

Peter You *are* going to be stripped naked, Ambrose. Last chance. Membership?

(**Ambrose** *remains silent.* **Peter** *nods.* **Jackie** *jumps forward and loosens* **Ambrose**'s *trousers, allowing them to fall to his ankles.*)

Now, Ambrose. You do look silly. I'm sure you feel silly. Do you? Which item would you prefer us to take off next, Ambrose?

Jackie The lot! Strip the bastard now!

Peter Ambrose, the ball's in your court. Wanna sign now?

(**Ambrose** *does not answer.*)

Very last chance, kid, before we bare you to the elements.

Jackie I'll strip everything off. . .

(He moves towards **Ambrose**, *but* **Peter** *motions him back.)*

Peter One! Last chance.

(Sings)

'Ambrose. You're gonna be stripped naked.'

I'm gonna do a count-down, Ambrose, and if you haven't responded by zero, I'm afraid it's tough luck.

(to **Jackie***)* Ready?

(To **Ambrose***)* Ready? Five. Four. Three. Two. One.

(Pause)

Zero!

*(***Jackie** *dives forward to remove* **Ambrose***'s underpants.* **Ambrose** *struggles.)*

It's all right! Leave it for a moment!

*(***Jackie** *steps back.)*

Ambrose, how far are you gonna carry on this charade?

Ambrose I'm not carryin' anything on.

Peter Are you not? Sit down.

*(***Ambrose** *moves towards the chair.)*

Not there. Just sit where you were standing.

*(***Ambrose** *hesitates.)*

Jackie He said sit down! *(Pushes* **Ambrose** *down by the shoulder, leaving him sitting on the floor.)*

Peter Alright now?

*(***Ambrose** *looks disgusted.)*

You don't really look comfortable. Lie back. Come on, make yourself comfortable.

*(***Jackie** *makes for* **Ambrose** *but he is already leaning back. He lies motionless on the floor.)*

Is that better? Yes, you look more comfortable now. Any complaints?

Ambrose My back's sore.

Peter His back's sore. No problem. I know an old Indian trick. Turn over on your stomach.

*(***Ambrose** *doesn't move.* **Peter** *steps forward and prods* **Ambrose** *with his foot once or twice.)*

That's it, roll over.

*(***Ambrose** *rolls over, flat on his stomach.)*

Right now, back-soothing time.

*(***Peter** *steps onto* **Ambrose***'s back. He walks back and forward, stopping to prod here and there.* **Ambrose** *winces in pain.)*

44

Is that any better Ambrose? The pain away yet?
(**Peter** *places one foot on* **Ambrose**'s *head. He applies some pressure.*)
Feel like doing a spot of writing yet, Ambrose? A couple of sentences or so?

Jackie   Trail him up and we'll knock his ramp in now.
(**Peter** *steps down off* **Ambrose.** **Ambrose** *immediately rolls over, pulls his trousers up, and gets to his feet.*)

Peter   Who gave you permission to get up? Oh, I see you wanna make a statement. How stupid of me, c'mon, sit down, Ambrose.
(**Ambrose** *sits on the chair.* **Peter** *hands him some paper and a pen.*)

Ambrose   Can I put on my shoes?

Peter   Why not?

Ambrose   And you told me there wasn't gonna be any violence.

Peter   You call that violence?

Jackie   Wait till we really start.
(**Ambrose** *puts on his shoes.*)

Peter   Now, what are you going to write for us?
(*Silence*)
Worked it out yet?

Ambrose   I've nothing to write about.

Peter   Take the prisoner to his cell.

Jackie   What? Let me knock his. . .

Peter   Take him away.
(**Jackie** *puts on his coat.*)

Jackie   Come on, ballocky Bill.
(**Jackie** *grabs* **Ambrose** *roughly to his feet.*)

Peter   Before you go, I want you to think about something.
Ambrose, I have tried, we have all tried, to show you the easy way out of this. Throughout three interviews you've had every chance to respond. From this moment onwards, it's a weeping and a gnashing of teeth. Somebody's gonna get hurt. Somebody has to lose. This system tends to produce losers.
See ya.
(**Jackie** *opens the door. He pushes* **Ambrose** *out and throws his coat after him.*
Peter *goes.*
Jackie *hands* **Ambrose** *over to* **Davy** *at the desk.*
Davy *puts* **Ambrose** *in his cell and locks it.*
Yvonne *enters.*)

Yvonne   I have been asked to ask you to help me shift some files from the back office.

(Davy *and* Yvonne *go.*
Ambrose *has been standing motionless in the centre of his cell.*
Suddenly he lashes out and kicks the chair over.)
Ambrose   Bastards! Bastards!
            (He moves quickly to the bed.)
            I'm not going through that again! No way!
            (He starts pulling the bed out from the wall.)
            At least not voluntarily anyway.
            Bastards!
            They can fight me for it.
            The next time they come for me they're gonna have to trail me out –
            unconscious!
            (He upends the bed towards the cell door.)
            Put up with that? Some chance!
            (He positions the bed to block the doorway.)
            I mightn't win but I'm not gonna stand around to be treated like a
            hunted animal.
            (He grips the chair and lifts it off the ground.)
            I'm gonna cleave the head off the first bastard comes through that
            door.
            (Shouts) The first fucker comes in this cell's getting the head cleaved
            off him! Man, woman or child!
            Come on!
            What's wrong with yiz?
            Scared?
            You yellow bastards!
            Yiz are all right in twos and threes, but there's not one of yiz man
            enough to stand up on your own!
Willie   Who's that, who's that?
Ambrose   Hey, fat ballocks! You down there! Come you down here and
            I'll start with you!
Willie   What?
            What'd I do, what'd I do?
            *(**Ambrose** puts the chair down and moves over to the bed.)*
Ambrose   Is that you, Willie?
Willie   No problem, Ambrose. Me, me, me.
Ambrose   What are you doing in here?
Willie   On holiday. Mini-weekend away from the troubles. *(Laughs)* All
            meals inclusive. *(Laughs.)*
Ambrose   But what have they you in for?
Willie   Nothin', nothin'. Picked on me for nothin'.

46

Ambrose   They picked on me too, Willie, but they've picked on the
wrong man this time. I've barricaded my cell. The first peeler comes
through the door's getting the head cleaved off him.
Willie   Magic, magic. I like, I like. Which hospital do you think they'll
take you to? *(Laughs.)*
Ambrose   I don't care. They're not gonna treat me like an oul' dog and get
away with it.
Here, Willie. Listen, Willie. If anything does happen to me, you
inform my wife as soon as you get out, will you?
Willie   No problem, no problem.
Ambrose   You won't forget now?
Willie   No problem. She'll be delighted to hear you stood up to the
Branchmen. Bully Ambrose. Magic, magic. I'll tell her, I'll tell her.
*(**Ambrose** comes away from the door slowly. A fresh thought has
struck him. He looks back round at the makeshift barricade. He
jumps back to the door.)*
Ambrose   Hey! Hey, Willie! Willie Lagan!
(He frantically trails the bed away from the door.)
Willie!
Willie   Yes, yes.
Ambrose   Listen, scrub what I just told you. Don't say anything to my
wife.
Willie   What?
*(**Ambrose** pulls the bed back towards its original position, up against
the wall.)*
Ambrose, what?
Ambrose   Willie, don't tell my wife anything. Forget what I just told you.
Willie   You drunk, drunk?
Ambrose   Look, listen. If you do run into Christine, Willie, tell her I'm
alright.
Willie   What about the barricade, what?
Ambrose   The barricade's away. Tell her you were talking to me and that
I said everything's alright. Will you do that?
Willie   Right, right, no problem, our kid. I'll see her.
*(**Ambrose** tidies up the cell. He stands the chair up, grips it
momentarily, then places it against the walls. **Willie** shouts.)*
Ambrose! Ambrose!
Ambrose   What?
*(**Davy** enters the cell corridor.)*
Willie   Are you, are you allowed to wank in here?
*(**Ambrose** falls on the bed laughing.)*

Davy   Alright, alright, shut it up down there.
   (He strides towards the cells and checks on the prisoners.
   Stanley, **Peter** *and* **Jackie** *enter the interview room.)*

Jackie   That Fogarty's a cheeky bastard. Asked me to try and get him a
   pen and a newspaper on the quiet.

Stanley   Peter, is he being kept isolated?

Peter   'Course he is.

Stanley   Definitely?

Peter   Definitely. Except. . .

Stanley   Except what?

Peter   Except, when I was returning him to his cell earlier on, that stupid
   idiot, Constable McFadden, allowed him to see another prisoner
   who knew him. It wasn't my fault.

Stanley   What?

Peter   Lucky enough, it's only that nut they have in for rioting. Lagan, his
   name is.

Jackie   That raker!

Stanley   Jesus Christ. I left specific instructions. How do they know each
   other?

Peter   I don't know.

Jackie   They live beside each other. I was looking at Lagan's statement.
   He lives in Grosvenor Place and our fella lives round the corner in
   McDonnell Street.

Stanley   Get him.

Jackie   What?

Stanley   Get the other fella.

Jackie   The raker, Lagan?

Stanley   Yes, get him over here straight away.

Jackie   Whatever you say.
   *(***Jackie** *goes to the cells.)*

Peter   What do you think?

Stanley   You never know. This fella might know one or two things about
   Fogarty that could be vital to us. You say he's being held on a riot
   charge?

Peter   Seems a bit flimsy to me. A load of young lads, you know, the usual
   mob, were attacking the Station yesterday after a protest march and
   one of the soldiers claims Lagan was in the thick of it. I mean, no
   matter how far you stretch it, he hardly fits the bill as an IRA
   godfather.

Stanley   Hardly, but we can make it stick if necessary. It'll do nicely as a

48

big stick to beat this fella with, to get some information out of him.

Peter I'm warning you, he's not the full shilling.

Stanley How many of them are?

    (**Stanley** *exits.*

    Davy *opens* **Willie**'s *cell door.* **Jackie** *enters the cell.*)

Jackie Right, Slim Whitman, let's have you on your feet.

    (**Willie** *jumps to his feet, both hands stabbling the air above him.*)

Willie I like, I like. No problem.

    (**Willie** *starts dancing round the cell, strumming an invisible guitar*
    Then he sings.)

    'Freedom is a word I rarely use
    Without thinking, without thinking.'

Jackie Don't be getting excited, Slim. You're only going for another interview.

Willie (*immediately forlorn*) Ah fuck, ah fuck.

Jackie (*taking* **Willie** *by the arm*) C'mon, let's go.

Willie (*bending down to lift his guitar*) What about m'guitar?

Jackie You can leave that. We're only going round the corner.

    (**Jackie** *and* **Willie** *leave the cell.*)

Willie I'm not being released then, no release?

Jackie Did you ever hear of Rudolf Hess?

Willie Yes, yes. Nazis. (*Salutes*) Hitler.

Jackie Well, you'll be stuck away that long, we're thinking of putting you in along with him.

Willie Ah fuck, ah fuck.

    (*Sings*)

    'Please release me, let me go. . .'

Jackie Shut up, you idiot, this isn't the Grand Ole Oprey.

    (*They enter the interview room.* **Jackie** *turns to* **Peter**.)

    Have you got a box of Aspros? You'll be eating them in handfuls before we're finished with this lad.

Peter Come in, Willie son. Sit down, make yourself at home. Smoke?

Willie Don't smoke, don't smoke, but I'd take a pint of double. (*Starts laughing*) A pint of double. I like, I like.

Peter Willie, if I had a pint of double to give you, I'd give you it.

Willie Would you fuck, would you fuck. You're a Branchman, peeler. (*Laughs*) I'm no mug!

Peter How do you know Ambrose Fogarty?

Willie (*thinks for a second*) Pass. Pass, by-ball.

    (**Willie** *roars with laughter.* **Jackie** *walks round and grabs* **Willie** *by the back of the hair.* **Willie** *lets out a yell.*)

Jackie Fun time's over, Willie! Answer the question!

Willie Alright, alright. Watch the head.

Peter Ambrose Fogarty, Willie?

Willie He lives round our way, McDonnell Street, round the corner.

Peter What does he do?

Willie Cheats at cards, cards up his sleeve.

Peter Besides cheating at cards, do you ever see him knocking about?

Willie Yes, yes. He knocks about with a big one from New Barnsley, separated she is, separated.

Jackie Listen. Do you realise the seriousness of this situation? You are in a police station and you're being asked questions by police officers. You can be charged with withholding information if you don't start answering questions.

Willie Okay, you win, you win. Ask me another. Fingers on the buzzers. *(Presses his finger on the table and laughs.)*

Peter Willie, I'm gonna ask you a serious question.

Jackie And we want a serious answer.

Willie Completely serious?

Jackie Totally serious.

Peter Is Ambrose Fogarty in a terrorist organisation?

Willie Yes.

Jackie That's more like it.

Willie Yes, he's a committee member of the Lower Falls Dart Team.

Jackie And they're terrorists?

Willie Well, they have me terrorised anyway! *(Laughs)* I'm barred from their club for life for calling the chairman a no-good, wasting, bastarding parasite!
Imagine! Life! I can't throw a dart ever again because I had a dopey row with the chairman, what, what?
Life? Isn't it just as well they're not the Government in power! They'd hang you for falling behind in your rent!

Peter I take it you don't like the chairman?

Willie Bastard, bastard. He brought me in front of the committee and sentenced me to life. Said I could appeal in 1990! Nineteen fucking ninety! Wee bastard. I fixed him, I fixed him.
(Laughs.)

Peter What did you do?

Willie Well, he owns this prize greyhound bitch, smashing dog, smashing dog, called 'Lightning Strikes', 'Lightning Strikes'. It's won its last eight races in a row at Dunmore. Three thousand pound, three thousand pound in prize money. Champion bitch, champion bitch.

50

Well, I climb over his yard wall in the early hours of the morning and mated his dog with our oul' mongrel, Rocky. *(Roars)* And any other oul' fleabeg there was knocking about too! *(Roars)* I soon made short work of 'Lightning Strikes'. He lets it run about the district now, like an oul' stray. *(Roars.)*

Peter Did he ever find out who did it?

Willie I suppose he has his suspicions! *(More laughter.)*

Peter Willie.

Willie That's me, that's me.

Peter Willie, I like your crack, but we still need one or two questions answered.

Willie *(sings)*
'There are more questions than answers.
And the more I find out – the less I know.'
Good singer, me, good singer.

Peter Willie, I'm gonna put you back in your cell now. But tomorrow the boss will be here and he won't be happy with all your jokes. He's a very tough man. So you'd need to answer any questions he asks you. Is that clear.

Willie Clear, clear.

Jackie Or it'll be that there. *(Holds up his fist.)*

Peter All right. You're not worried then?

Willie Worried?
(Gets up, plays an imaginary guitar and sings)
'It takes a worried man to sing a worried song
(Moves towards the door.)
It takes a worried man to sing a worried song
It takes a worried man to sing a worried song
I'm worried now
But I won't be worried long.'
*(**Willie** leaves followed by **Jackie**. **Jackie** slaps **Willie** on the back of the head.*
Peter *gathers his papers and exits.*
Willie *and* **Jackie** *reach the cells, where* **Davy** *is waiting.)*

Jackie Lock this maniac up, will you.
*(**Willie** starts singing. 'It Takes a Worried Man' again as **Davy** locks him up.)*
Here, open this door a minute. I want a word with this man.
*(**Davy** opens **Ambrose**'s cell door. **Ambrose** is sitting on his bed. His eyes fix on the door at the sound of it opening.)*
Good news for you, Fogarty, I just thought I'd call in and let you

know. We've just interviewed your cell neighbour.
Bit of a Country-and-Western singer. In fact, he's a very good singer.
He seems to have a lot to say about you. What is it they say in the
movies? 'He's singing like a canary.'
(*Black-out*)

Act Three

Yvonne *enters and approaches the interview room door. She has her arms wrapped around a number of folders and papers, clutched to her chest.*
    As she reaches to open the door, Captain Levington *enters nearby, rather slyly. Just as* Yvonne *enters the room and turns on the light, the* Captain *sneaks up behind her, knocks the light off and slips his arms round* Yvonne's *waist.*
    Yvonne *is completely taken by surprise and shock.*

Captain   Hello, Yvonne.
    *(*Yvonne *squeals and jumps forward out of his grasp before looking round to identify the* Captain.*)*
Yvonne   Good God, Colin! You frightened the life out of me. Put the light on quickly!
Captain   *(moving towards her)* Don't be in such a rush, kid.
    (He takes the papers off her and sets them down on the table.)
Yvonne   What are you doing, Colin?
Captain   Nothing that doesn't come completely natural to me.
    (He puts his arms around her.)
Yvonne   Please, Colin, someone'll be coming in here any minute for those papers.
Captain   There's no one here now.
    (By now, the Captain *has edged* Yvonne *back up against the door. He leans his mouth forward to kiss her.)*
Yvonne   Not now, Colin.
    (He kisses her. She responds and they kiss and embrace passionately. Yvonne *breaks off.)*
    Please, Colin, not now.
    Someone's bound to catch us on. I'll. . .
    (He kisses her again. She again responds. He then begins to touch and caress her body. She breaks away again.)
    Oh Colin, please!
    (He forces another kiss. Suddenly a loud noise is heard nearby. It

sounds like a door slamming.)
Someone's coming.

Captain   Shit!
*(**Yvonne** immediately breaks away from the **Captain**, turns the light
on and hurries to the other side of the room.)*

Yvonne   It's all right for you, I work here.

Captain   But there's no one coming. Listen, it's quiet again. Come on,
Yvonne.
(He makes advances again. She moves away.)

Yvonne   No. No. Not now, Colin. Later, some other time.

Captain   Like when?

Yvonne   Later.
(She opens the door.)

Captain   Where are you going?

Yvonne   I'm only leaving the door open in case someone comes. They'll
see we're only talking.
Anyway, you should be able to control yourself until Friday
night.

Captain   Yeah.

Yvonne   You did say you were taking me to the stock-car racing?

Captain   Yeah, I know what I said.
(He lights up a cigarette.)

Yvonne   You mean it's off?

Captain   I didn't say that. When did you say it was?

Yvonne   Friday night.

Captain   You off?

Yvonne   I can arrange it.
Colin?

Captain   Yeah.

Yvonne   Do you still mean what you said, I mean earlier, when you
talked about the summer?

Captain   Oh crikey. What do you think? Do you think I just go about
telling lies?

Yvonne   No, of course not. I'm not saying that. It's just that. . . well. . . I
am very serious about travelling.

Captain   I told you. There are four hotels. Two in France and two in
Spain. My brother's out there now.
I mean, I'm only here because my dad insisted on me getting a good
grounding in the Army, before going into the family business.
This is my last month, in two weeks I'm off.

54

Yvonne   You've still to leave me the address.

Captain   Yeah. Like, if you did decide to come over, you would have to work hard.
Dad isn't the type to allow even his own family favours. If anything, he works us harder.

Yvonne   I wouldn't mind hard work.

Captain   It would probably only be receptionist or something but at least you would be eating.
And seeing a bit of the world.

Yvonne   Not to mention the sun.

Captain   Not to mention the sun.

Yvonne   This is ridiculous. Absolutely ridiculous.

Captain   What is?

Yvonne   I bet that if I really did arrive down on top of you in some hotel in France, you'd turn and run the other way.

Captain   Don't talk rubbish. Look.
(He produces a picture and shows it to her.)
If you arrive before the 25th, you'll get me there.

Yvonne   Where's this?

Captain   A place called Marseilles.
It's down south.

Yvonne   I know where Marseilles is.

Captain   Well anyway, after the 25th I could be anywhere. But I don't think you've any real intentions of leaving this place in the first instance.

Yvonne   Wanna bet?

Captain   Yvonne, I've met your type a dozen times before.
Big ideas. Big plans. And big mouth.
You can't just walk away from this job and you know it. Your old man won't let you for a start.

Yvonne   I make my decisions.

Captain   You're just a plain, simple, Irish girl who'll never see any further than her nose, never mind the South of France.

Yvonne   I'm not Irish.

Captain   Well, you're not fucking English.

Yvonne   Don't be so bloody ignorant, Colin.

Captain   All right, I'm only joking.

Yvonne   I don't see the funny side of it. And I didn't like the way you just came storming in here, pawing over me, I'm not. . .

Captain   Alright. I'm sorry, I'm sorry. Don't get your knickers in a twist.
Must get back now, duty calls. I'll see you on Friday night then?

Yvonne   You might.

Captain   Oh my God, I said I was only joking.

(**Yvonne** *remains indignantly silent.*)

Wait a minute. I know what's wrong with you. Yeah.

Not only are you afraid to leave this bloody place but I suspect you're still attached to that carrot-face – Constable McFadden.

Yvonne   Maybe I am. Maybe I am. I don't see how that's any of your business.

(**Davy** *enters and walks towards the interview room.*)

Captain   Poor Yvonne. I can see it all in front of you. You'll marry carrot-face, have a couple of kids and live happily ever after in bleeding, boring Belfast.

Yvonne   I might just do that.

Captain   Yes, Yvonne love, you just do that.

(**Davy** *enters the room. The* **Captain** *turns, walks into* **Davy** *and smiles broadly.*)

Hello, Davy!

(*The* **Captain** *exits.*

Davy *stares at* **Yvonne** *for a moment. He sees the two undone buttons of her shirt.*)

Davy   Sorry I missed the party.

(**Yvonne** *hurriedly does up the buttons.*)

Yvonne   Oh Davy, I was. . . I was just in here leaving in some papers when the Captain. . .

Davy   Yeah, it looks like that.

Yvonne   Don't be stupid, Davy, the Captain. . .

(**Davy** *turns sharply and exits.*)

But Davy. . . Davy!

(*She stops in the room for a few seconds, looks perplexed, then hurries off stage.* **Sergeant Knox** *is at reception, using the radio.*)

Knox   Bravo Hotel, Bravo Hotel to Five One, over. Bravo Hotel, Bravo Hotel to Five One, over.

Radio   Hotel, send, over.

Knox   Five One, would you go to the owner of the chip shop referred to earlier and inform him that his car has been located in Alpha Quebec's patch, over.

You might also inform him that we were unable to recover the box of pasties he was going on about.

Radio   Will do, roger out.

(**Davy** *enters.*)

Knox   Davy, take over here for a while, till I go and find Yvonne, will you?

Davy   Check the soldiers' sleeping quarters.

Knox   And what sort of a remark is that to make?

Davy   I've just. . . Do you know what I've just. . . Ach, it doesn't matter. She'll get her come-uppance with that character.

Knox   I take it you're talking about the Captain?

Davy   Who else?

Knox   I agree with you about him but I think you're being very unfair to Yvonne.

Davy   I don't.

Knox   I suppose that tone of voice suggests you haven't managed to get her to go out with you again?

Davy   It's not for the want of trying. I've asked her dozens of times. I've went out of my way to coax her, but she won't wear it.

Knox   Maybe that's your problem.

Davy   What?

Knox   Trying too hard. Maybe it's time to ease off a wee bit and then she might begin to wonder.

Davy   I don't know now if I even want to see her again.

Knox   Ach, I wouldn't let it get me down. You best bet is to let Yvonne run on for a while. I guarantee you she'll not be long catching herself on.

Davy   She's gone past that stage.

Knox   Look, didn't she say she was going to the stock-car racing on Friday night?
Your move is to turn up there with big Veronica out of Drugs, and act like you're having a great time.

Davy   Big Veronica out of the Drugs Division?

Knox   The very one.

Davy   Oh, I couldn't do that. That would cause problems.

Knox   How?

Davy   I like a wee smoke of marijuana myself, now and again.
(Both men laugh. **Knox** *goes.* **Peter** *and* **Jackie** *enter from the street.* **Jackie** *looks at the incident book while* **Peter** *lifts a file from a table.)*

Jackie   To tell you the truth, I was glad to see her going in. She had me up half the night, every night for a month. Hiya, Davy.

Peter   I know the feeling.

Jackie   How many have you now?

Peter   One boy and one girl and it's more than enough.

Jackie   That's my fourth.

Peter   Jesus Christ.

Jackie   Feeding time in our house is like a religious ceremony. They eat

57

as if it was the Last Supper. Now you know why I volunteer for all the overtime I can get.

Peter Better than Sirocco, eh?

Jackie Don't talk about that place. I only stuck it eight weeks, after my da speaking for me and all. There was blue murder in the house over it.

Peter Your father worked in Sirocco too?

Jackie Thirty-one years. *(Imitates voice)* 'You have to go out and earn a living wherever you can get it,' he kept saying.

Peter What did he say when you put on the uniform?

Jackie Shocked. A bit shocked, but as pleased as punch in the end. Although my mother has done nothing but worry from the day and hour I signed up. The wife takes it a bit more philosophically. She reckons I'm so thick-skinned, a bullet would bounce off me.
(Peter and Jackie go. In his cell, Ambrose jumps up from the bed and paces the floor.)

Ambrose What the hell's keeping them? My third day and no interrogation yet? It must be the early hours of the morning now. Something's up.
What about Willie?
'Singing like a canary'? I wonder is he still there.
(He goes over to the cell door.)
Willie! Willie Lagan!

Willie That you, Ambrose?

Ambrose Willie. Did they mention my name in your last interview?

Willie Not once, no.

Ambrose Are you sure, Willie?

Willie Definitely, definitely, not once, no.

Ambrose So what do you think they're gonna do with you?

Willie Don't know, don't know.

Ambrose Ah, they'll probably release you anytime now.

Willie What about, what about you, what's happening?

Ambrose Ah, they're trying to pin a dopey oul' charge on me.

Willie What, did you kill somebody, Ambrose, what?

Ambrose *(chuckles)* You know me better than that, Willie. I couldn't kill anybody if it was to save my life.

Willie Ambrose.

Ambrose What?

Willie 'Member, 'member the time you broke your leg running away from the soldiers in Albert Street? *(Laughs)* Great crack, great crack. Like it? Crack, crack?

Ambrose I can assure you, Willie, it wasn't funny at the time.

58

(Loud laugh from **Willie.***)*
Willie   Na, no joke, no joke.
*(***Davy** *enters the cell area.)*
Ambrose   Willie, you won't forget to see Christine when you. . .
Davy   Alright, alright, wrap it up. That's the last time you two's being warned!
Willie   Why, what are you donna do, Quaseemoto, lock us up? *(Laughs.)*
Davy   That's enough in there.
Ambrose   Maybe they're gonna execute us, Willie!
Davy   I said that's enough!
*(***Peter** *and* **Jackie** *enter the interview room.)*
Jackie   Have you ever shot anybody, Peter?
Peter   Have you?
Jackie   You don't have to answer if you don't want to.
Peter   You tell me, then I'll tell you.
Jackie   No. No, I haven't. Closest incident was in Cromac Street two years ago. We got a call to the Post Office. We arrived just in time to see the guys turning the corner into Eliza Street. I fired one shot and just as the two guys disappeared an elderly woman stepped out onto Cromac Street. Bullet went straight through her shopping bag. Two fuckers got away.
Peter   Close enough.
Jackie   Too close. And you?
Peter   Yeah, I've shot somebody.
Jackie   Badly wounded?
Peter   Dead.
Jackie   Dead!
Peter   Oh, it was a long time ago. I was only about twenty-one at the time. A guy was climbing over a wall after planting a bomb in a factory. There was a bit of a gun battle and I shot him. Once in the head and once in the chest. Not bad for a nine-millimetre Browning at forty-five yards.
Jackie   It must have been rough for you.
Peter   Not really. It's all part of the job. Same as a joiner uses a saw, I use a gun. Can't do the job without it, in fact.
Jackie   Not in this country anyway.
Peter   Don't kid yourself. It's the same all over now. There's a violent crime every six minutes in New York. Los Angeles City Morgue is that overcrowded they've had to build racks up the walls to accommodate all the murder victims.
Violence is now a way of life. Look at John Lennon, Reagan, the

Pope. The world's going mad. A cop can't do his job without a gun anymore. The only place they're not robbing and shooting each other on the streets, is fucking Russia!
(Stanley enters.)
Stanley   Right, Jackie, fetch Willie Lagan for us.
(Jackie moves towards the door.)
Peter   Bring a gun with you. You never know what's liable to happen.
Jackie   I think I'll manage.
(He goes.)
Stanley   What are you talking about?
Peter   I'm just pulling his leg.
Stanley   Well, I want you to pull Willie Lagan's leg. Right out of its socket if necessary.
Peter   Oh, exciting.
Stanley   We're only twenty-four hours left. Fogarty must be made talk. So what we need from Lagan is a signed statement implicating Fogarty in IRA activities. When we hit him with that he'll be ours for the taking.
Peter   No holds barred?
Stanley   No holds barred. I'll join the proceedings if necessary.
Pete   No problem, Stanley. It's as good as done.
*(Stanley goes. **Davy** opens **Willie**'s door and **Jackie** enters.*
***Willie** is prancing about the cell, imitating a monkey, grunting and shrieking.)*
Jackie   What in the name of Christ!
*(**Willie** grunts and shrieks. He jumps onto the bed.)*
Come on, Willie, it's interview time.
*(He moves forward and takes **Willie** off the bed by the arm.)*
What are you playing at?
Willie   Monkey, monkey. If I'm gonna be caged up, I might as well act like a monkey!
*(He jumps about under **Jackie**'s restraint.)*
Jackie   Well, come on round to the interview room and we'll see if we can get you some bananas.
Willie   Guitar, guitar. Take my guitar with me?
Davy   Your guitar'll be all right here, nobody'll touch it.
Willie   *(singing as he leaves the cell)*
'And as they marched him to the scaffold
His head he proudly held up high.
Brave Willie Lagan, we salute you
And we never. . .'

(Jackie and Willie enter the interview room.)

Willie You still here, still here? Have they not got you a break since yesterday? That's cat, bad, bad.

Peter Don't you worry about me. It's yourself you need to be worried about.

Have you decided what you're going to tell us?

Willie Yes. A joke, a good joke. Tell you a good joke, not long, not long.

Man says to me, 'Willie, my wife's an angel.'

I says, 'You're lucky, mine's still living.'

(Laughs.)

One more, one more.

Doctor's surgery, Doctor's surgery. Packed, crowded.

I walks in and lets off a big fart, big fart.

Man says to me, 'Willie, how dare you fart in front of my wife.'

I says, 'Sorry, I didn't know it was her turn.'

(Laughs.)

I like, I like, I like! 'I didn't know it was her turn'!

(He forces a handshake on **Peter** *and* **Jackie***.)*

Magic, magic. Every one a gem.

(Another fit of laughter.)

'I didn't know it was her turn'!

Peter Willie. At nine o'clock tomorrow morning you will be taken to Townhall Street and formally charged with drunk, disorderly and riotous behaviour, as a result of which you will spend six full months in Crumlin Road Prison.

Willie *(stops abruptly, then bursts out laughing again)* I like, I like, I like. Good joke, good joke. Know any more?

Jackie Think this is fun, do you?

(He moves towards **Willie** *aggressively.)*

Peter Just let him get the giddiness out of his system for a moment or two.

(Pause.)

Are you finished yet, Willie?

Willie Yes, yes, finito.

Peter Ready to answer a few questions?

Willie Yes, yes. Fire away. Hold on, hold on. What's the star prize? A car, a car? No. No. A year's supply of dummy-tits? *(Laughs)* Right. Fingers on the buzzers.

(Jackie bangs **Willie***'s fingers.)*

Sore, sore.

Jackie I said, the fun's over!

Peter If you remember, Willie, we were talking about Ambrose Fogarty, a neighbour of yours. Remember?

Willie   Yes, yes.

Peter   Now, Willie, I want you to tell me everything you know about him.

Willie   Like what, like what?

Peter   Well, everybody knows he's in the IRA. Have you ever seen him with a gun?

Willie   *(jeers)* Ah! Have I ever seen him with a gun? I know what you're at. You want me to become a Brussel!

Peter   A Brussel?

Willie   Brussel sprout – tout!

Peter   Look at it this way, Willie. Are you working at the moment?

Willie   Yes, yes.

Peter   What are you doing?

Willie   Good job, good job. I'm a hod carrier in a marshmallow factory. *(Roars.)*

Peter   Seriously, Willie, are you working?

Willie   No work, no work. Paid off.

Peter   On the Buroo?

Willie   That's right, that's right.

Peter   That couldn't be very much each week.

Willie   Bad, bad.

Peter   I can offer you a substantial sum each week just to give us little snippets here and there on people like Ambrose Fogarty.
Now there's no need to worry. Nobody has to know except us. We'll pay the money to you any way you want. Anywhere you want. *(**Willie** thinks it over.)*

Willie   Nobody'll know?

Peter   Not a sinner.

Willie   Every week?

Peter   Without fail.

Willie   How much, how much?

Peter   How much would you want?

Willie   Am, a. . . a. . . hundred pounds a week, tax-free and four weeks holiday a year.

Peter   I'm serious, Willie. We could send you out a cheque for twenty pounds every week.

Willie   Twenty pounds a week? I'm serious too. That's way below the union rate, too low, too low.

Jackie   Union rate?

Willie   If I brought that to the Regional Secretary of the Northern Ireland Touts' and Informants' Union, they'd laugh at me. No way, twenty pounds a week! Touts' Union wouldn't wear that, wouldn't wear it.

(Peter takes out twenty pounds in five-pound notes and counts them out on the table.)

Peter   Now, Willie. There's twenty pounds on the table and there's the door.

If you tell me of just one incident involving Ambrose Fogarty, that twenty pound'll be in your pocket and you'll be out through that door in five minutes.

What about it?

Willie   Can't do it, can't do it. Don't know nothing, nought.

Jackie   I don't think he needs the money at all. If he's signing the Buroo and he says he plays the guitar and sings in the clubs, then he's all right for a few bob.

In other words, he's breaking the law.

Peter   That's right, two sources of income.

Jackie   Illegally claiming benefits.

Peter   Worth a year in jail, eh Willie?

*(**Willie** remains silent.)*

Got you this time, have we?

Jackie   If you don't come across with some talking inside two minutes, the boss is going to be here and you'll be in serious trouble.

Willie   Can I say something, what?

Peter   Go ahead.

Willie   All right, I won't play the clubs anymore.

Peter   That's very good of you.

Jackie   Too right, you won't.

*(Suddenly the door bursts open and **Stanley** enters.)*

Stanley   Has he told you anything yet?

(He throws his coat off, rolls up his sleeves and sets his watch on the table.)

Peter   Not a thing.

Jackie   Only jokes.

Stanley   Is that right? Stand up!

*(**Stanley** trails **Willie** up.)*

Willie   Watch the coat, watch the coat.

*(**Stanley** strikes **Willie** with a fierce punch to the stomach. **Willie** bends over and **Jackie** pushes him to the ground. **Stanley** and **Jackie** trail **Willie** back onto the chair. **Willie** is in considerable pain.)*

Stanley   Know any jokes now, do you?

*(He punches **Willie** again.)*

Prepared to talk yet? We'll soon see.
What is it this man has in his cell with him?
Jackie   A guitar and a parcel of bread.
Stanley   *(to* **Peter***)* Away and smash up the guitar.
*(***Peter*** goes to the cells to fetch the guitar.)*
Willie   Listen, listen. Don't touch my guitar, please, please.
Jackie   Well, are you gonna start talking?
Stanley   Is Ambrose Fogarty in the IRA?
Willie   Yes, yes, he probably is.
Stanley   Never mind probably. Is he or is he not?
Willie   I'm not sure, I don't know.
*(***Jackie*** punches **Willie***.)*
Yes, yes, he is!
Stanley   I'm sure you've seen him doing something at some time or
another?
Willie   Don't think so, don't think so.
*(***Jackie*** punches him.)*
Stanley   Ever see him with Sean McAlister?
*(***Willie*** shakes his head. **Jackie** strikes him.)*
Willie   Yes, yes. I did.
Stanley   When?
Willie   All the time.
Stanley   When? This week, last week, the week before, when?
Willie   I can't remember exactly.
*(***Jackie*** hits him.)*
Two weeks ago, aye, it was two weeks ago.
Stanley   What were they doing?
Willie   Nothing, nothing.
*(***Jackie*** strikes him.)*
Jackie   What to fuck were they doing, Lagan?
Willie   Nothing, I swear.
Stanley   You're a liar!
They must've been doing something. Walking, talking, in a club, in a
car, what were they doing?
Willie   Nothing.
Jackie   Answer the question!
Stanley   Eh?
Willie   In a car, in a car.
Stanley   Where?
Willie   Bottom of our street.
Stanley   Doing what?
64

Willie Nothing. They just got out of a car at the bottom of our street.
(**Peter** *returns with* **Willie**'s *guitar.*)
Stanley Right, sonny, if you don't start talking within five seconds, I'm smashing this thing to smithereens.
Willie Please, please, don't hurt my guitar, please.
Stanley What did they do when they got out of the car?
Willie Nothing, I swear, nothing.
(**Stanley** *holds the guitar up and throws it to* **Peter** *at the other side of the room.*
Willie *attempts to move but is restrained by* **Jackie**.
Peter *throws it back but* **Stanley** *lets it fall to the ground.*)
Willie Ah fuck, ah fuck.
(**Stanley** *walks over and raises his foot above the guitar.*)
Stanley Are you going to answer the question?
Willie They fired a rifle, but it was just in the air, just test-firing I think, know, trying it out.
Stanley And they just got back into the car and drove away?
Willie That's right, that's right.
Peter How did you know it was a rifle, Willie?
Willie I don't know. All's I know, it banged like fuck.
Peter Did it fire one shot at a time or a whole lot quickly together?
Willie Yes, yes, there was a right lot.
Peter Like a machine gun?
Willie Yes, yes, like a machine gun. Frightened the balls off me.
Peter (*to* **Stanley**) There's your machine gun.
Stanley Yeah.
Willie Do you mean they were using yours? Cheeky bastards!
Stanley I don't suppose you're prepared to appear in court, Lagan, to testify to what you've just told us?
Jackie Or sign a statement?
Willie Ah fuck, I'm still young yet. Too young to die. Too young.
Stanley We could drop all the charges against you.
Willie Let me think about it, what. Think, think.
Stanley Take him back to his cell.
Willie Am I being released now, what? Know like, I've told you all about Fogarty, the lot. I must be up for release.
Stanley We'll have to wait to see how we go with Fogarty.
Willie I might be released?
Stanley You might.
Willie Magic, magic. Shake, shake.
(*He offers to shake hands.*)

Stanley *(to* **Jackie***)* Take him away.

*(***Willie** *jumps up and grabs his guitar.* **Jackie** *opens the door.)*

Stanley Do you play that thing at all?

Willie No, I don't!

*(***Jackie** *pushes* **Willie** *out and both men go to the cells.)*

Stanley That could be the break we are looking for.
A stupid oul' fool from round the corner has neatly wrecked
Ambrose's wee shop.

*(***Stanley** *and* **Peter** *leave the stage.* **Jackie** *hands over* **Willie** *to* **Davy**
and leaves the stage.

Davy *locks* **Willie** *up and goes.*

Willie *starts banging on his cell door.* **Ambrose** *hurries to his own cell
door.)*

Willie I want out! I want out! I want. . .

Ambrose Willie! Willie!

Willie Yes, Ambrose.

Ambrose You alright?

Willie I'm alright, but they beat up my guitar, smashed it.

Ambrose Why did they not release you?

Willie Why is the earth round – how the fuck do I know why they didn't
release me?

Ambrose Willie! Willie, did they mention me this time?

Willie Mention you? Who do you think you are, Yasser Arafat, what?

Ambrose Are you sure?

Willie Calling me a liar, what, what? I'm in jail too, you know. Got the
works, the lot, filled in.

Ambrose You were beat up?

Willie Ambrose, there's one of them a madman, mad he is. Why, why do
they do it, Branchmen, eh?

Ambrose Now you've asked a question, Willie. Why are Branchmen
Branchmen?
It's all to do with the system, Willie. Do you know what the system is,
Willie?

Willie Yes, yes. I'm constipated myself at the minute, bad, bad.

*(***Stanley** *and* **Peter** *arrive at reception.* **Stanley** *checks out something
on the incident book.)*

Stanley He's bound to cave in when we throw this stuff at him.

Peter I can't wait to see his face.

Stanley I can't wait to smash his face.

Peter Strange, but I couldn't help feeling a wee bit sorry for your man
Willie Lagan there.

66

Stanley What do you mean?

Peter Ach, nothing really. Just a wee bit sort of sorry to see him getting knocked about.

Stanley Well don't. He won't feel sorry for you or your wife and children if you get a bullet in the back from one of his cowardly neighbours. Like Ambrose Fogarty.

Peter Now, there's a man I have no sympathy for. This is effectively our last chance to put him away.

Stanley That's if you don't break down feeling sorry for him in the middle of it.

Peter Not with this fella.

Stanley Well, we can't do it without getting him to make a statement and putting pen to paper. You know what half of these judges are like. By the way, what was the report on those things you were checking out?

Peter Not terribly beneficial, I'm afraid. There was a pub off Ann Street that had its toilets replastered but the owner only knew one of the workers as Sean.

We couldn't ascertain one way or the other whether any roofing repairs were carried out in Glenhill Park and when we visited the McAlister house the parents were very hostile. Just said the sons weren't in and if we wanted them why didn't we go looking for them.

Stanley Good enough. Get Jackie and let's get under way.

(**Yvonne** *enters the cells area pushing a trolley. She stops beside* **Ambrose**'s *cell.*)

Yvonne Could I have this cell opened, please?

Davy It's opened.

(*She enters the cell and lifts the plate and cup, watched closely by* **Davy**. *Embarrassed, she pushes the trolley on to* **Willie**'s *cell.*)

Yvonne It's got very warm in here today, hasn't it?

Davy I'm alright.

(**Davy** *unlocks* **Willie**'s *door.*)

Your dishes?

Willie No problem, no problem.

(*He hands them over.*)

Is that my girl? It is, good, good, good. Coming in for a lumber? What? A nice big lumber, me and you? A couple of smacks of the rubbers, what?

Davy Alright, back inside.

Willie Toilet, toilet, I wanna use the toilet.

Davy In a minute, in a minute.

Willie That's two minutes. Said it twice, twice.

Davy Very funny. Just hold on a minute till we get sorted out and I'll come back and let you go to the toilet.

Willie No problem, no problem.

(**Davy** *locks the cell door.*)

Yvonne That's the lot, isn't it?

Davy That's it.

(*She turns the trolley and moves off.*)

Yvonne I'll see you later then.

Davy See you.

(*She stops near the exit.*)

Yvonne By the way, in case you're still thinking what you're thinking, you've got it all wrong.

Davy I'm not thinking anything.

Yvonne You accept then that nothing went on between me and the Captain in that room?

Davy Huh!

Yvonne Do you, Davy? This is important to my job. I don't want anybody running around this station talking about me.

Davy Yvonne. I don't *care* what went on.

Yvonne And another thing. I have to work with you, so there's no point in me and you continually fighting the peace out, is there? I want us to be friends.

Davy Friends? We were supposed to be engaged in a fortnight's time.

Yvonne Okay, so it's not as formal as that anymore, but that shouldn't stop us being good friends.

Maybe we could even go out for a drink to the Sports Club sometime.

Davy (*sarcastically*) How does this Friday night suit you?

Yvonne Davy. Listen, Davy. . .

Davy No, you listen to me for a change.

I had feelings for you. Strong feelings. But you decided, in your usual, arrogant way to tramp all over them.

Not only did you tramp on them but you jumped on them, danced on them and kicked them.

Now. Strong and all as my feelings were, I'll never feel the same again for you after what I've seen of your behaviour over these last few days.

Yvonne, I mightn't have the social status you're looking for, but I've got principle. You? You're a. . . you're no better than a whore.

(*She immediately slaps him on the face.*)

A sign of guilt if ever I saw one.

Yvonne Don't you ever accuse me of anything, Davy McFadden!
When I want lectured on morality and men you're the last person I'll
go to.
You walked into that room and immediately thought the worse. I
can't help it if your twisted little mind is sex in the brain.
But I'm not in the habit of having it off with men in police stations or
anywhere else.
And I'm certainly not a whore.
If that's what you're looking for, you'll find plenty of them down
around Dee Street.
(She turns to leave.)
Davy Yvonne?
(She stops.)
Fuck off.
(She goes. **Willie** *bangs his cell door, realises it is opened and steps
out of his cell.* **Davy** *swings round and sees him.)*
Willie You never locked the cell door, never locked it.
Davy How the bloody hell!
(He rushes down to **Willie** *and ushers him back into his cell.)*
Willie Toilet, toilet? Go now, go now?
Davy No, you bloody well can't!
(He slams the cell door shut and locks it.)
Willie *(sings)* 'Please release me, let me go,
For I can't hold it in anymore. . .'
*(***Stanley** *enters the interview room.* **Jackie** *arrives at the cells to fetch*
Ambrose *while* **Peter** *hands in a document to* **Sergeant Knox** *at
reception.)*
Knox Oh, there you are. I was wanting to inform you that there have
been several enquiries about Mr Fogarty, in fact his wife hasn't been
off the phone. And his solicitor wants in to see him as soon as
possible. You know what Jones is like.
*(***Peter** *shrugs his shoulders.)*
It is my duty to report those facts to you.
Peter You've reported them.
(He turns to move on.)
Knox But what'll I tell his wife or anybody else that rings?
Peter What everybody else is told. He's still helping police with
enquiries.
*(***Peter** *walks on to the interview room.* **Jackie** *arrives
with* **Ambrose**, *leaves him in the interview room and immediately
goes.)*

Peter   Sit down, Fogarty.

Stanley   Stand up!

Peter   Do you know how long you've been in here now?
(**Ambrose** *shrugs his shoulders.*)
Over sixty hours. Know how many people have enquired about you?

Stanley   Not one. Not a ruddy sinner.

Peter   Your wife hasn't been seen, nor heard of, since your arrest. Your
so-called comrades haven't bothered their backsides either.

Stanley   No statements in the paper, no protests. They haven't even
bothered to get you a solicitor.

Peter   Do you get it, Ambrose? Nobody gives a fiddler's. Not one person.

Stanley   What do you do all this for? The cause?
You joined to further the cause. You worked hard, you did your
duty, you did everything that was asked of you.
You gave up a lot of your own time. No doubt about it. Ambrose
Fogarty has been an excellent volunteer. A twenty-four-hours-a-day
man.

Peter   Risked his life and freedom many's a time. The last time of course,
being only a fortnight ago on the Andersonstown Road.

Stanley   And what for? To be forgotten about inside three days. You're
sitting here facing fifteen years while your 'idealistic' comrades are
bevvying away in one of their many drinking clubs.

Peter   Yes, but his leaders stand by him.

Stanley   Oh, aye. The leaders! The leaders haven't even got the guts to live
in Belfast. They just make the odd sortie up North to make a few fiery
speeches, urging all the young lads on the Buroo from the Falls Road
to attack the Brits.

Peter   And then they fuck off to the safety of Dublin.

Stanley   And it's left to fools like Fogarty here to do the dirty work.

Peter   And end up in jail.

Stanley   Or dead.
Answer me a question, Fogarty. How many of your Dublin GHQ
staff have ended up dead while attacking the enemy on the streets of
Belfast?
Come on. Name me one? Just one?

Peter   And there haven't been any frantic phone calls from Dublin
enquiring about him.

Stanley   Not at all.

Peter   It's about time you wised up, Ambrose. Once you step inside this
police station, you're on your own. Your family, friends and
comrades don't care.

'Did you hear Ambrose Fogarty got fifteen years? God, that's terrible. Make that four pints of Harp and two vodkas, Harry!' *(Laughs)*

It's a joke, isn't it.

Stanley   If it wasn't so damn serious.

When you're not working for McAlister, what else do you do?

Ambrose   Sign on.

Stanley   Wouldn't you know.

Peter   That was a foregone conclusion.

Stanley   Here's a man who opposes Britain tooth and nail, wants Brits out and all the rest, yet he's over to the Social Security office as quick as the next to claim British money.

Ambrose   There are no jobs.

Stanley   Only bank jobs eh?

Why don't some of you go out and get jobs and earn an honest, decent living?

Ambrose   I told you, there are no jobs. There's nearly fifty per cent unemployment round our way.

Stanley   And why's that? Because people like you have been doing their best to wreck the economy since 1969.

Ambrose   The figures were nearly as bad before 1969.

Stanley   Don't talk nonsense.

Ambrose   Who's talking nonsense? Northern Ireland has traditionally been an unemployment blackspot.

Heightened by the fact that unemployment has been concentrated in Catholic areas. Ballymurphy, thirty-five per cent, Ballymena, two point nine per cent.

Where's the nonsense there? That's the facts.

Peter   A right old politician we have here.

Stanley   Did you not know? Fogarty is a failed student. Two years at Queen's University was too much for him.

Ambrose   I didn't like University. I left to get married.

Peter   You plumped for a career in terrorism instead.

Ambrose   I'm not a terrorist.

Stanley   You're not a Franciscan monk either.

Peter   Are you interested in politics?

Ambrose   Suppose I am.

Peter   Well, what do you believe in?

Ambrose   Am I being charged because of my political views?

Peter   No.

Ambrose   Then, I'd prefer not to discuss my politics.

Stanley   Listen, sonny, don't try and be clever in here. You know rightly you're not in here because of your political views. You're in here because of your decision to use violence and robbery to further those views.

Ambrose   I disagree with using violence for anything.

Stanley   Huh! Who do you think you're talking to – a foreign press reporter? That line doesn't wear in here. We know a bit more about the likes of you than the world's press does.

Ambrose   I have nothing to hide from anyone.

Peter   You're hiding your politics.

Ambrose   I'm not.

Peter   Then tell us what you believe in. Are you a Republican, a Socialist, a Unionist, a Conservative, or what?

Ambrose   Do you know what you are?

Peter   Yeah, of course.

Ambrose   I'm sure I don't have to ask what your politics are.

Peter   No, I'll tell you. I vote middle of the road.

Ambrose   Middle of fuck.

Peter   I'm telling you I do. He doesn't.

Stanley   No, I vote for the Big Man. And I don't only vote for him, I keep him informed on certain matters – goings on, inside the police.

Ambrose   Bit of a mole.

Stanley   I regard it as doing my duty. For God and country. It's only my duty.

Peter   What do you think of the Big Man, Ambrose?

Ambrose   I think, that if this was a normal country inhabited by rational human beings, far from being a leading politician, he would be a traffic attendant on the Lagan towpath. Only allowed to open his mouth when he got hungry.

(Stanley immediately stands up.)

Stanley   Do you know that in his personal life, he is a warm, friendly man. I've never met a man with more compassion and understanding. He is a man of strong principles, is impeccably honest and insists on he same from all those around him.

Ambrose   So is the Ayatollah Khomeini.

(Stanley sits down.)

Peter   Who's your hero then? Chairman Mao?

Ambrose   I don't indulge in heroes. Life's not made up of heroes. It's made up of ordinary unsung people trying to search out a living.

Peter   And you're on the side of the ordinary-downtrodden-man-in-the-street.

Ambrose   You're learning.

Stanley   What were the unfortunate victims that died in La Mon?

Ambrose   I told you before. I detest the use of violence but since you
mentioned it, the victims in La Mon were exactly the same as the
victims on Derry's Bloody Sunday. Ordinary, innocent, decent
people.

Peter   Are you suggesting two wrongs make a right?

Ambrose   Not in the slightest. I'm just reminding you of things it seems
you prefer to forget. Selective retention, I think the sociologists call
it.

Stanley   Nobody can blame the police for La Mon or Bloody Sunday.

Ambrose   No, but you can be blamed for the death of young Michael
McCartan on the Ormeau Road recently. Not to mention Devenny
and Rooney in '69.

Peter   1969 was a long time ago.

Ambrose   Yes, but the men who did the damage are still in the RUC.

Stanley   Who the hell do you think you are! Sitting there pontificating
about the country's police force. And you a bloody bank robber! A
person who steals off other people!

Ambrose   That's untrue.

Stanley   What's untrue about it? Are you still going to sit there and tell me
that you didn't collaborate with Sean McAlister to organise and
carry out the robbing of a bank on the Andersonstown Road on
Thursday the 6th?

Ambrose   You know rightly I didn't

Stanley   We know rightly you did. And better still you know we know.
And there you are sitting as if butter wouldn't melt in your mouth.

Peter   Where were you on Thursday the 6th?

Ambrose   Again?

Stanley   Just do what you're told. You got up at what time?

Ambrose   Well. . . I was only. . .

Peter   Remember, Ambrose, we have in front of us the story you told us
yesterday. So you'll need to get this right – word for word. Minute by
minute.

Stanley   The truth this time.

Peter   If you don't get it right, we can do you for withholding
information.

Ambrose   Well. . . I started work around twelve or so and worked till. . .
I think it was well after two.

Peter   And?

Stanley   Speed up these answers, we haven't got all day.

Ambrose We had lunch then in the White Fort Inn on the Andersonstown Road.

Stanley How far away is that from the bank?

Ambrose Which bank?

Stanley Answer the question!

Peter The one nearest the pub!

Ambrose I'm not sure.

Stanley You're a liar!

Peter You're at it again, Ambrose.

Ambrose I'm telling you the God's honest truth.

Peter You're not. Inside twenty-four hours you've changed your story about your movements.

You said the last time you started at eleven and finished at one. Now it's, started at twelve and finished at two.

That's the third time you've told a different story.

Ambrose It's hard to remember exact times.

Stanley I suppose then you wouldn't remember what you did the night before Thursday the 6th?

Ambrose The night before. . .

Stanley With our friend McAlister.

Peter At the bottom of Grosvenor Place?

Ambrose I can't really remem. . .

Stanley Answer the bloody question!

(He bangs the table with both hands and gets to his feet.)

I've had just about enough of this.

Peter We know you test-fired a sub-machine-gun that night.

Stanley We have witnesses.

Peter You can't deny this one.

Stanley Did you or didn't you?

Ambrose Of course not, I was. . .

Stanley You did! We know you did.

Now, I want you to write down on that piece of paper everything that happened over those twenty-four hours.

(He shoves a pen and paper in front of Ambrose.)

I don't care if you say you only drove the car or did look-out or whatever, but you better sign for something.

You're not walking out of here m'boy. No way.

Peter You're better facing up to that now. If you sign, you could get off lightly. If you don't sign, we'll hold you personally responsible for planning and organising the entire operation.

As I said before – anything up to fifteen to twenty years.

74

Stanley   This is the last time I'm going to do this.
   (He places the pen in **Ambrose**'s *hand.)*
   If you don't start writing this time I'll not be responsible for what
   happens to you.
   (The room door opens slightly.)
Jackie   *(behind door)* Has he not signed yet?
   *(***Peter** *jumps up from the table and moves to the door.)*
Peter   It's all right, leave it for another few minutes. He's going to sign
   now.
   *(***Peter** *closes the door.)*
Stanley   Well, Fogarty?
   *(***Ambrose** *moves his hand slowly to the top of the page. He stops,
   drops the pen on the table and sits back.)*
Stanley   What the hell are you doing?
Peter   You're asking for trouble.
Stanley   Are you going to sign, Fogarty?
   (He moves over to **Ambrose** *and starts shaking him by the shoulder.)*
   Sign it, sign it, sign it!
   (The door suddenly bursts open. **Jackie** *enters, throwing off his coat
   and rolling up his sleeves.)*
Jackie   Where is the bastard?
   I'll soon knock the nonsense out of you mate!
   Get on your feet!
   Get on your feet, I said!
   (He trails **Ambrose** *to his feet.)*
   You won't sign, eh!
   (He punches **Ambrose** *fiercely in the stomach.)*
   We'll soon see about that.
   *(***Stanley** *grabs* **Ambrose**'s *arms from behind.* **Jackie** *repeatedly
   punches him and yells abuse.)*
   Bastard! Cunt! Cunt! Bastard!
   *(***Ambrose** *finally falls to the floor, taking blows from both* **Jackie** *and
   ***Stanley**. **Peter** *sits calmly on the table.)*
   Get up you cowardly bastard!
   *(***Jackie** *and* **Stanley** *trail* **Ambrose** *to his feet.* **Stanley** *stands ready.
   ***Jackie** *walks round and round* **Ambrose**.*)*
   You're a cunt. What are you? A cunt!
   Cunt, cunt, cunt!
   (He grabs **Ambrose**'s *arm and twists it, forcing* **Ambrose**'s *head to
   the floor.)*
   Who robbed the bank? Answer me!

Answer me, cunt!
Admit you took part in robbing the bank.
Tell me! Tell me!
(**Jackie** *is almost hysterical.*)
You're a thieving cunt, what are you?
Cunt, I asked you a question.
What are you? What to fuck are you?
Answer me! Answer me!
Don't you think you're getting away this time, mate. You've another twelve hours to go and I'm just going to beat the ballocks off you for twelve solid hours.
Got that? Have you got that? Do you not hear me talking to you, cunt? Are you deaf as well as stupid?
Do you fancy this for twelve hours?
And let me tell you this.
(*Reaches down with his free hand, grips* **Ambrose** *by a lock of hair and marches him to the end of the room*)
If you don't admit and sign before those twelve hours are up, we'll just walk you outside this station and rearrest you all over again. Just like that.
Only this time, it'll be a seven-day detention order, eh? Fancy that, cunt? Do you fancy that? Fancy that, fancy that, fancy that?
(*Grips* **Ambrose**'s *hair in two hands, holding him on his tiptoes*)
By fuck, I'll bring you down to size before I'm finished.
Isn't that right, cunt? Cunt, cunt, cunt, cunt, cunt, cunt, cunt, cunt! Isn't that right?
Now (*trails* **Ambrose** *by the back of the hair onto a chair by the table*) we are going over to sign a confession.
You, mate, lift that pen and write down in detail what we all know happened.
Lift it!
Lift the pen.
(*He shakes* **Ambrose**'s *head.*)
I said (*bends* **Ambrose**'s *head right down to the table and bangs his face against the paper on the table three times*) lift that pen!
(*Holds* **Ambrose**'s *face crushed against the table*)
You've got five seconds to lift that pen, cunt.
Five seconds.
(*He shakes* **Ambrose**'s *head. After a few seconds,*
Ambrose *brings his right hand up onto the table and searches for the pen. He finds it, pauses and then throws it*

across the room.)
Bastard!
(Jackie *and* **Stanley** *both set upon* **Ambrose,** *eventually leaving him in a heap in a corner of the room.)*
Stanley   *(to* **Peter)** Take him back to his cell.
(Peter *moves over and supports* **Ambrose** *to his feet. He walks him to the door.)*
Fogarty!
(Peter *and* **Ambrose** *stop.)*
I'm arranging immediately for a seven-day detention order for you.
(Peter *and* **Ambrose** *go out.*
Sergeant Knox *is at the desk. The telephone rings. He lifts the receiver.)*
Knox   Yes, Bill. . . probably around three o'clock. . . right. . . 'bye.
(He *puts the receiver down.* **Ambrose** *and* **Peter** *arrive.)*
Peter   Take this prisoner back, Sergeant, please.
Knox   Right.
(Shouts back) Yvonne, keep your eye on the desk!
Yvonne   *(off-stage)* Okey dokey!
(Peter *goes to the interview room.*
Knox *escorts* **Ambrose** *to his cell.)*
Knox   Lock this man up.
Davy   Right Sergeant.
(To **Ambrose)** In you go.
(Ambrose *turns to* **Knox.)**
Ambrose   I want to make a complaint, Sergeant.
Knox   What about?
Ambrose   I've just been beaten up.
Knox   Get me some paper, Davy. Let's go inside.
(Davy *fetches some paper from his table.* **Ambrose** *and* **Knox** *enter the cell.)*
Knox   You want this to be a formal complaint?
Ambrose   As formal as you can make it.
(Davy *hands in the paper.)*
Knox   Thanks, Davy. Right, what happened?
(Knox *sits down.)*
Ambrose   Two members of the RUC have just systematically beaten me up.
Knox   How do you mean beaten?
Ambrose   How do I mean? Sergeant, why do they do it?
(Stanley, Peter *and* **Jackie** *are in the interview room.* **Stanley** *paces*

up and down.)
Jackie I wouldn't mind being a disc jockey.
Peter *(laughs)* Catch yourself on.
Stanley I wouldn't do anything else.
I know I'm doing something worthwhile. Not only is it the right thing, but so many people are depending on us doing a good job. When an old-age pensioner gets mugged, who is it investigates? Us. When people get their cars stolen, who is it treks round for hours looking for them? Us.
What happens when people use violence to gain political objectives? We've to search out the culprits and get them in front of the courts. Us! It's left to the police.
(The dialogue is intercut between **Ambrose**'*s cell and the interview room.)*
Knox I suppose somebody has to do it.
Ambrose Sergeant, what sensible, level-headed person would work at a job which entailed punching other human beings on a daily basis? 'I had a hard day at work today love, is the tea ready? I punched the fuck out of ten people today.'
Who would do it?
The only other people I know who do that for a living are boxers. But Muhammed Ali earned twenty million pounds over twenty years, how much will the average cop earn in a lifetime?

Peter And a fat lot of thanks we get too.
Stanley Of course, it's not the money. I would earn more working on the nightshift in Michelin's.
But it makes you wonder why mavericks like Fogarty actually do what they do for no money.

Knox I don't know, son, but there's a lot of bad boyos comes in here. I'm not saying you're one, but they must have you in for something.
Ambrose That's right. I've come this far because I believe in something. I had good prospects before the Troubles started. Now I'm living on Social Security.
I wouldn't allow myself to go through this if I didn't believe in something. An ideal. Sergeant, I believe that the people of this place can live in peace and prosperity under a new social order.
They're my reasons. I'm not in this to buck my own goat. Those other guys lift a pay cheque at the end of the month. For what? For beating up people?

78

Christ, it's a sick society that can throw up police stations where people are beaten up systematically.
And a sick police force that carries it out.

Peter   But is there no other legal way of getting convictions against the wild men?

Stanley   Quite simply, no.
Most of them are hardened operators who come in here knowing the whole set-up inside out.
While we can't get witnesses to stand up in court, these jokers know it's only a matter of sitting the three days out.
Peter, what's a few slaps around the face if it keeps the likes of the Shankill Butchers, or the people who carried out the Whitecross Massacre, safe from the community, behind bars?
Don't we have a duty to put those people behind bars with whatever means is at our disposal?

Ambrose   How many innocent people have been beaten up in here through mistake or suspicion?

Knox   That's impossible to tell. I just look after my end of things by filling in any complaints that are made and sending them on.

Ambrose   Sending them on to who?

Knox   All complaints are investigated by senior police officers.

Ambrose   What? Do you mean to tell me that my complaint against the police is going to be investigated by the police themselves? What would have happened if Watergate had been investigated by Richard Nixon?
Ask my brother am I a liar.
Forget about the complaint, Sergeant. No one's going to tell me that this place isn't simply a conveyor belt for putting people through the courts in order to prop up a rotten system.

Stanley   It's a contribution to peace.
Putting all the gunmen behind bars is the final result.
Everyone's sick of violence. The community wants peace.

Ambrose   Huh, peace! Outside the word 'love', 'peace' must be the most abused word in the English language.
Isn't it funny how a government only wants peace when it's the government?
There is no such thing as a pacifist. Who was it threatened an eye for an eye?

Stanley And love thy neighbour.

Ambrose Unless he's of a different religion.

Stanley Do unto others as you would have them do unto you.

Ambrose Only do it first.

Stanley Jackie, go and instruct Sergeant Knox to release Fogarty.
Jackie Looks like he's slipped through our fingers.
Stanley I'm afraid so.
Jackie Think we'll ever get another chance?
Stanley Ambrose Fogarty? His sort always come back.
Jackie What about the other fella, Lagan?
Stanley You don't have to ask me that.
Jackie Right.
> (**Jackie** goes.
> **Willie** starts singing as the next series of events takes place.
> **Jackie** arrives at the desk.
> **Peter** and **Stanley** leave the interview room.
> **Knox** leaves **Ambrose** to be locked up and goes to the desk, where **Jackie** tells him **Stanley**'s decision.
> **Knox** returns to the cells, takes **Ambrose** out, gives him his personal effects and shows him to the front exit.
> On his way back, **Knox** comes across the **Captain**, who is in civvies and carrying a grip.)
Knox Where are you off to?
Captain A place called England. Bermondsey, to be exact.
Knox But aren't you. . . I thought you and Yvonne were going out this Friday night.
Captain Yvonne? Sergeant, I hope to be getting drunk down my local this Friday night.
> (He moves towards the exit.)
> And every other Friday night, if I can help it. Six years is a long time in the Army. See ya.
Knox But don't you want to go in and say cheerio to her?
Captain You do that for me, Sergeant, would you?
> (He smiles broadly and exits. **Knox** moves off stage.
> **Davy** opens **Willie**'s cell door.)
Davy Right, Willie, you're leaving here now, let's go.
Willie Magic, magic. I like it, I like it.

(He grabs his things and makes for the door.)

Davy Not so fast, not so fast.

*(**Davy** and **Willie** move towards reception.)*

Willie Magic, magic. Hear the one about the man was collecting money down our street?

Holds out a collection box and says to me, 'Dr Barnardo's Home.' I says, 'I didn't know he was away!'

(Roars with laughter)

'I didn't know he was away.' I like, I like.

Davy I don't know what you're laughing at. There's a vehicle waiting at the front gate to take you to Townhall Street.

You're being kept in custody to face three separate charges in Court on Monday morning.

Willie Ah fuck, ah fuck.

*(**Willie** drops his parcel of bread, spilling the pieces of soda farl out onto the stage.*

Black-out)